Dee Dee,

I was really lucky that you came along just as I was getting deeply involved in this Central history project. Your interest, encouragement and support meant a lot and kept me going. And your reading of the first draft was a real ray of sunshine. Like so many things, this book owes a lot to my association with you. Thanks.

Dick

A Competitive Spirit

The Story of
Central Bank of the South

Richard H. Gamble

Printed in the United States of America by Birmingham Printing and Publishing Company.

ISBN# 0-961-80910-8

ISBN# 0-961-80911-6 Softcover

Library of Congress Catalog Card # 86-072920

Dedication

THIS BOOK IS DEDICATED to the future! Specifically, to the future of Central Bancshares of the South. I believe that how well we carve out our future can be influenced by how well we remember our past.

If our next generation of leaders and employees follows the same simple game plan recorded in this book, they will enjoy even greater success than those of us who have gone before them.

Central should never be intimidated by larger financial institutions. Our success against them is well documented. The Central organization is built to survive and endure if we always strive to give our customers a better deal than our competitors do.

The safest ticket to long-term prosperity is market penetration. That calls for an outstanding sales force backed up by a highly motivated support organization. The foundation is in place; all we need to do is to keep repeating what has worked so well in the past. Since working is fun, when it's working, Central should continue to be a fun place to work.

HARRY B. BROCK, JR.
Chairman and
Chief Executive Officer
Spring 1987

Table Of Contents

Foreword

THIS HISTORY OF CENTRAL BANK of the South gives concrete reinforcement to the fact that, despite our computers and mathematical models, banking remains a "people game."

It shows how a handful of highly motivated people could start a new bank in the face of powerful, long-established competitors; how it could price its services to take advantage of its newness and of the difficulties established banks would have in matching its policies, and how it grew by relying on its human touch, its personal contact between the top officers and the staff and especially on the willingness of its directors to take a central role in its marketing and expansion efforts.

Do politics and effective lobbying play a role in the growth of a bank and especially in the way banks are organized? Read this work and you will be assured that effective contact with individual lawmakers is a key to what has changed banking in Alabama and in the rest of the nation as well.

The irony of Central is that its hard times, as elaborated in this book, resulted from its efforts at liability management and other techniques that diverted attention away from its emphasis on person to person contact.

Here then is a volume that helps to explain why, despite mergers, acquisitions and over 150 bank failures in 1986 alone, there has been an increase in the number of banks in the last decade, not a shrinkage. For new banks continually are being chartered, and many of them prosper because they, too, concentrate on the human touch that built Central from an idea to a major force in Alabama in less than two decades.

PAUL S. NADLER
Professor of Finance,
Rutgers University and
Contributing Editor,
American Banker

Preface

A HISTORY, CHAMELEONLIKE, takes on characteristics of its subject, so this is an unorthodox history of an unorthodox bank. From the outset, all parties agreed that this account should be the *story* of Central Bank. To this end, some scholarly baggage has been left behind and some statistical data stripped away so the story can move forward in a lively fashion.

Because Central compressed so much corporate living into 23 years, it has a story to tell when most of the principal actors are still alive and remember their roles. The oral accounts of more than 100 individuals (most of them preserved on tape in Central's archives) contribute to this story. Memories are fallible, but an occasional detail misremembered is a small price to pay for the kind of truth that can be told in the candid, first-hand accounts of the people who lived the events.

Memories are confirmed and augmented by a full written record. Both Central and State National Bank in Decatur kept meticulous minutes of board meetings, and the 1968 lawsuit that followed the hostile takeover of State National resulted in a wealth of depositions being taken from key figures and private documents being put in the public record. Few historians have such an abundance of primary information to use.

Central sponsored this history but gave the author unusual leeway to follow trails wherever they led, to talk with enemies as well as friends of the bank, to recount its failures as well as its successes. Central chose to be recorded as it has lived: conspicuously, with more vitality than caution. While this account is not completely unexpurgated, I think most readers will find it satisfactorily complete and uninhibited.

While I take full responsibility for the conclusions and blemishes contained in this volume, the sharp details are possible because I received first-rate help from more people than I have space to acknowledge. The text indicates where much of the information comes from, but does not mention Jo Prince of First Alabama Bancshares, Sue Morris of the Alabama Bankers Association, Laurie Dean of the Birmingham *News,* Cindy Rasco of Central's legal department, Mike Bean of Central's accounting department, Elizabeth Roy of Robinson-Humphrey/American Express or Charles Carlyle of Sterne, Agee & Leach, all of whom tapped their special sources of information to supply me with crucial data. Deirdre Parker's early reading of the manuscript and Nora Shea's late reading of page proofs were particularly helpful. Bradford McFadden, Jr., was my cooperative employer at the time I was dividing time and loyalty between his company and Central's history.

Preparing the history inevitably became a family project. Special credit is due to Paul Gamble, a seasoned historian who showed me the way and improved the manuscript; to Karen, my wife, true partner and reliable sounding board; to Jennifer, who patiently typed and filed, and to Ben, who lent not only his time but his computer to the cause and carried me across a technological threshold.

The fountainhead of knowledge for this story is certainly Central Bank, where Lloyd Rains, Terry Brannon and Carolyn Robertson became major resources, used repeatedly and with increasing respect for the depth and detail of their knowledge, for their candor and for their cooperative spirit.

Finally, there is Brock, the creative center of Central Bank, who remembers the details so vividly because he lived them so intensely, who laid out his mistakes for me almost as willingly as his triumphs, who made history and then saw that it could be told in an accurate, candid fashion.

Richard H. Gamble
March 2, 1987

Introduction

IN 1962, CENTRAL BANK of the South was a vague, unnamed idea in the imaginations of a couple of restless, ambitious men who had not even spoken of it to each other. By 1982, it had become, for the time being, the largest bank in Alabama. Twenty hustling, daring, arduous, enduring years had made it a financial powerhouse. Its founders and directors hit the streets to make the bank grow, and it made them rich. Its sole chief executive, a converted salesman steeped in the magic of Dale Carnegie, shaped the bank to fit his own notions of competition, service and excellence, and it made him powerful — and controversial.

Central Bank marched to its own drummer. It overran the complacent, outraged the traditional, tried the unthinkable, challenged and taunted the mighty. Brigades of lawyers fought a celebrated two-year legal war over the bank's most controversial gambit, but in the end, it did not make legal history. It fought tooth and nail for its future against a hostile, united banking industry in the legislative halls of Montgomery in one of the fiercest lobbying battles in memory, yet it was unable for a decade to pass legislation it wanted.

Still, it inspired fear and gratitude, admiration and resentment. It won notable victories and made conspicuous mistakes, and it paid dearly for its daring. But it grew with a vigor and vitality that would not be contained by the old forms and structures. And in the end it changed forever the face of banking in Alabama.

It prevailed because it was shrewdly directed, because it invented solutions when it could not find them, and because its people were zealots who worked with a joy and conviction that larger, richer organizations could not match.

As a bank, its history is a complex accretion of financial and personal transactions: deposits placed, loans made, bonds traded, budgets prepared, contracts signed. But in the beginning, there was the simple clarity of three dissimilar men whose paths converged almost by accident, men who embodied the three sets of qualities that would bring greatness to the enterprise.

There was Hugh Daniel, the soft-spoken man of integrity, the respected civic leader, the influential builder who became a patient investor, steady booster and temperate board chairman. Hugh Daniel was looking for a bank that would open on Saturdays.

There was Schuyler Baker, the canny, ambitious attorney, the inquiring legal mind and resourceful opportunist with keen political instincts and close ties to an Alabama political dynasty. Schuyler Baker was seeking clout and in spite of mounting frustrations, remained determined to found a bank.

Finally, there was Harry Brock, the rambunctious redhead, the irrepressible salesman, the hard-driving competitor, the shrewd strategist, the motivator of men, who was growing restless as a banker working in the shadows of older men bound to tradition.

◇

In 1962, Birmingham had five banks. The mighty First National Bank, founded in 1873, dominated banking in Alabama. Its deposits of $431.7 million accounted for 60 percent of the Birmingham market. Birmingham Trust National Bank, founded in 1887, had $175 million in deposits, a 24-percent share.

The Exchange Security Bank (1928) held deposits of $64.5 million, almost 9 percent of the city's deposits, while the Bank for Savings (1923), with almost $48 million in deposits, held a 6.5-percent share. The small, family-owned Steiner Brothers Bank (1888) reported deposits of less than $3.5 million, roughly half of 1 percent of the market.

Two banks held over 84 percent of the city's deposits, and there had not been a new bank in Birmingham since the

Security half of Exchange Security was founded 18 years earlier.

◇

In 1963, Birmingham came apart at the seams. Blacks protested, boycotted, demonstrated, rioted. Crosses were burned, then stores. Public Safety Commissioner Eugene "Bull" Conner turned the firehoses on demonstrators, then turned loose the dogs. Governor Wallace defied President Kennedy over segregation. Four young black girls were killed in church on a Sunday morning in the most lethal of the bombings that rocked the city.

White businessmen and civic leaders negotiated with black leaders to end the conflict, then were themselves called traitors and threatened with violence and boycotts by fervid segregationists. A new city government contended for power with an old city government that refused to leave. The parks were all closed.

An ugly reputation for violence and racial intransigence spread quickly that summer. "Case History of a Sick City" proclaimed the headline of a *Newsweek* analysis. *Look* featured Birmingham in "I Saw a City Die." Birmingham was at its lowest ebb.

CHAPTER ONE

The Spark

THE SPARK AND TINDER to start a very different kind of fire came together one June day in 1963 in an unlikely place: the office of Milton Andrews, president of the Bank for Savings. Schuyler Baker, then counsel to the state Alcoholic Beverage Control Board in addition to his law practice, had come by to talk over some ABC Board business with Andrews, its chairman. When he learned that Andrews was still tied up in a meeting of the Bank for Savings board, Baker sat down at Andrews' desk to wait for him.

The Bank for Savings was in the process of being acquired by Birmingham Trust National Bank. That merger was the brainchild of Frank Plummer, who had come to Birmingham in 1958 as BTNB's chief executive. BTNB was an ultra-conservative bank, but Plummer, a New Yorker, was a dynamic, progressive banker. He would soon be forced out of BTNB by dissatisfied directors but would go on to become the greatest merger maker in Alabama banking history, architect of the state's first multibank holding company, a formidable rival to the Central Bank leaders and the driving force behind the creation of another phenomenal Alabama banking organization, First Alabama Bancshares.

The Bank for Savings merger was Plummer's first big deal. It brought BTNB $48 million in assets and reduced the number of substantial banks in Birmingham from four to three, concentrating more than 90 percent of the city's deposits in the two big banks, BTNB and the First National Bank of Birmingham. This merger also upset some people and indirectly led to the organization of Central Bank.

Baker was waiting for Andrews, but the man who appeared in the doorway was Hugh Daniel, a Bank for Savings director. Daniel was a gentleman who never lost his temper, but Baker could tell that he was annoyed. There, as Baker recalls it, the following conversation took place.

"Schuyler, I want to talk to you."

"Fine, come on in."

"You've heard about this merger between BTNB and the Bank for Savings?"

"Yes, everybody knows about it, Hugh."

"Well, I think that if this merger goes through, it will eliminate Saturday banking in Jefferson County."

"I think that's true."

"I think that someone will start a new bank if that happens."

"I think you're exactly correct."

"I thought that you, with your connections in Montgomery, might know who it is."

"I do. It's me."

"It's you, Schuyler?"

"That's right. I have a charter for Birmingham and one for Bessemer."

"I'd like to be a part of it."

"Good, Hugh, because you've just ensured its success."

"Now there are two or three things I'd like to see happen. It's going to have to offer Saturday banking. The people need it. There are a lot of people who can't get to the bank except on Saturday."

"I agree with you. I'm 100 percent for that."

"I also think that no one should own a concentrated amount of it. It ought to be distributed as widely as possible throughout Jefferson County and Alabama. No one should own more than 10 percent of the bank except directors."

"That's fine. I agree. But Hugh, people are talking about grass growing in the streets of Birmingham. It may be very difficult to raise money. I would hope that you would underwrite or take more than that."

"All right, I will underwrite up to half of it, with the understanding that I will distribute it and not retain any more stock than anybody else."

"That's fine. That will ensure its success."

"Who are you going to get to run it?"

"I have someone in mind, but I'd like to talk to him before I tell you who it is. I don't want to compromise him in any way."

"That's all right. I think I can guess who it is."

"Well, Hugh, if you guess with me sitting behind Milton Andrews' desk, you're going to make a bad guess."

◇

The man Baker had in mind to run the new bank was not Milton Andrews, whom he knew would soon sign a non-compete agreement and retire from Birmingham banking, but a young executive vice president at the $66-million Exchange Security Bank who was already attracting attention with his bold business development efforts. When Baker placed the crucial call a day or two later, the phone rang at Harry Brock's desk.

For Baker, finding out that Hugh Daniel would back the new bank was the second piece of good news he'd had in the past year. Together they spelled the end to a long, frustrating effort by Baker to start up a bank. The first good news was the election of George Wallace as governor of Alabama in 1962.

Baker had been selling shoes in his native Huntsville in 1939 when he decided he wanted something better. He had lackluster high school grades and no money to pay for college, but he made the trip to Tuscaloosa to talk with the dean of admissions at the University of Alabama. The dean observed that Baker was no scholar and that it took money to go to college. Baker told the dean that he would sit in his outer office and starve until the dean found a way to admit him. The dean found a way, and Baker stayed to get a baccalaureate degree in law. After traveling the highways of Indiana for several years as an investigator for an insurance company, he settled in Birmingham in 1949 and started a law practice. He came to make a fair living as an attorney, but his ambition kept pushing him to find something better. He was not content to be what he calls a "skid-mark lawyer." He wanted to be a bank attorney.

Baker had been trying for years to get approval to start a bank during the Folsom and Patterson administrations. But the Federal Deposit Insurance Corporation would tell him he needed approval first from the state banking department, and the state banking department would tell him that they could act only after he had FDIC approval. "I felt like a ping-pong ball," he recalls.

Once he progressed far enough to get approval for a charter and began to raise the money to capitalize a new bank, but he ran into trouble when one of his backers was found to have a misdemeanor on his record and his banker friend Andrews told him, "I gave a bad report on you because of who you were going to hire to run it." Discouraged, Baker returned the money he had raised and quit — for the time being.

As a student at the University of Alabama, Baker had managed the campaign of a fellow student who won a campus election from a feisty boxer from Clio named George Wallace. Wallace wanted Baker on his side when he ran for governor, he said. Baker and Wallace became friends, and when Wallace did run for governor, Baker became his Jefferson County campaign director and started stumping for him. One of the men he publicly debated during the campaign was Harry Brock, a supporter of Ryan DeGraffenried of Tuscaloosa, a fraternity brother of Brock's and the choice of many educated urban professionals as the best hope to bring a progressive approach to Alabama politics. But Wallace beat DeGraffenried in a run-off contest to get the Democratic nomination, then went on to win the election. DeGraffenried was later killed in a 1966 plane crash.

Baker ended up with a promise of bank charters in Birmingham and Bessemer if he could raise enough capital and hire a good staff. He had already drummed up promises to buy approximately $400,000 of stock in the venture when he ran into Daniel.

Baker wanted to start a bank primarily for business and professional reasons, but like many other residents of Birmingham, he had his own little gnawing resentment at treatment by the big banks in town. When Baker had been ready to build a house, he signed up a bonded contractor, then went to his own small bank to seek a construction loan. He was sent to the First National Bank of Birmingham because it was "the only bank in town that makes that kind of loan." At First, he was told that the loan committee would consider his application at its next meeting — one month later.

Weeks later he was hailed and congratulated by the loan officer for having his loan approved. There was one stipulation, however: he had to move all his accounts to First. Baker balked. None too politely, he told the officer what he could do with the loan. You'll never get it anywhere else, he was warned. Nobody else makes these loans. You'll borrow from us or you won't get the money at all.

Baker would be damned if he didn't try. He went over to Exchange Security Bank, where an accommodating officer soon arranged the loan for him. "Are there any stipulations?" he wanted to know. "Just one," Harry Brock told him: "that you shake my hand."

So when Baker picked up the phone after his conversation with Hugh Daniel, he called Brock.

As Baker recalls their conversation, he told Brock he was going to start a bank, and Brock replied, "The timing is good, but why are you telling me? Our bank would be a competitor."

Baker replied, "I'm calling you because you are going to run it."

"I'm going to run it? Why would I leave the job I have here?"

"Just hold your horses a minute, Harry. Has anyone ever come to you and offered to shape a bank around you, just like a tailor fits a suit of clothes to you?"

"No. But I like the idea and I bet you could get the charter."

"You'd better believe I can. Of course you can stay where you are if you want to. You'll be well paid, but you won't really have any stake in the game. This would come with stock options, and I think you could do a good job at it."

"You're selling me. Who have you got with you?"

"I'm only going to name one name. If that doesn't mean anything to you, then forget the whole thing."

"Who is that?"

"Hugh Daniel."

"No kidding! Is Hugh Daniel with you? Where are you? I'll meet you at The Club in five minutes."

By the time he arrived at the private dining club, Brock was already there waiting, Baker recalls.

Brock had not really planned to leave Exchange Security to start Birmingham's first new bank in 19 years, but he had toyed with the idea of what he would do if he ever started a bank. After Baker relayed the ground rules he and Daniel had established (the Saturday hours and the widely distributed ownership), Brock agreed to them and quickly moved on to his own concerns.

There should be no deadwood on the board, he told Baker. Directors would be partners in the venture and would give the bank not only all their own business but would actively solicit business from friends and business associates. The bank needed a working board, not a display of prestige. They discussed the initial board, according to Brock. It would include Brock, Baker, and, if he could be persuaded to join them, Daniel. Baker wanted to add his brother-in-law, insurance agent Stewart Welch. Brock proposed Dr. Wendell Taylor, an orthodontist who had straightened his children's teeth. He also suggested automobile dealer John Israel and contractor Frank Hardy. These men would in fact make up the original board and work together as the Central team for more than 20 years. (Daniel died in 1983, but the others are still active supporters of the bank in 1987 as this history goes to press.)

Baker told Brock that he had already placed about $400,000 worth of stock. "Let me take care of the rest," Brock told him. "I think I can offer it to people who will deposit in the bank two or three or five times the amount of stock they get."

"That's what I want you for," Baker agreed.

It was part of Brock's plan, he recalls, to offer the remaining stock only to people who would bring business to the bank. Stock placement was his first big opportunity to build a fired-up bank. He was going to use it as bait: the more business you promised to bring to the bank, the more stock you'd be allowed to have.

The whole conversation with Baker at The Club, Brock recalls, took 15 minutes. Although Brock had still not met Daniel, the essential elements of Central Bank had come together. It had no name yet, and only three men in all the world knew it existed, but it was more than an idea now. It was a plan.

◇

Brock was a gregarious country boy who grew up on a farm near Hokes Bluff, where going into town meant driving seven miles to Gadsden, Ala. He was friendly and fun-loving and played softball with enthusiasm but no great ability. People there knew him and liked him, but nobody figured him to be a world-beater. After a stint in the Navy submarine service near the end of World War II, he went to the University of Alabama in Tuscaloosa, where his accounting professor noticed nothing remarkable in the strapping redhead but his marketing professor was impressed by his sales presentations. He also played on the University golf team.

Roommates grumbled that Brock would come in late, grab a beer and a banana and settle down on a couch to study but promptly fall asleep. He would get up in the morning and do as well on exams as those who spent half the night studying. He is remembered more for his high spirits than his high ambition.

After graduating in 1949 he married Jane Hollock of Birmingham and returned to an unassuming life in Gadsden where he worked for his father, an oil distributor, driving trucks, repairing equipment and painting service stations. He left his father's business and, over a two-year period, sold cars and advertising and in 1953 wound up in Rochester, N.Y., as a salesman for Socony Vacuum Oil Co. During those years, the

Brocks had babies and saved their pennies for a washing machine.

One day Jane noticed an ad in the Gadsden paper for a Dale Carnegie course. She believed that her husband's future did not lie in driving trucks or selling oil, so she convinced him that the washing machine could wait, that he should use the money to take the course. He did, and it was like getting religion. Brock went on to train as an instructor in the Dale Carnegie program and taught the courses himself through much of his career.

He was becoming an exceptional salesman in Rochester but not a northerner. When Norman Pless, an old friend and the executive vice president of the Exchange Bank in Birmingham, offered Brock a position at the bank, he took it and happily returned to Alabama in 1955 where, with Pless' help, he set out to learn banking. It was, in some ways, an odd pairing, the fun-loving automobile and petroleum products salesman and the conservative banking institution. Brock had paid little attention to credit and finance, and banks in 1955 were not known for their energetic sales and marketing. It was soon apparent, however, that Pless knew what he was doing.

Old Brock friends like G. W. "Red" Leach, a Gadsden insurance agent, saw a definite change in their old buddy. "He just loved it. He really found his niche with banking. It was a challenge he could work with," Leach observes. "The frustration didn't come along until later."

Brock set out to learn all there was to know about lending. Much of his education was internal — from Pless and others at Exchange Bank — but Guy Caffee, a contemporary of Brock's and later the CEO of Birmingham Trust, recalls having Brock as one of his students in an American Institute of Banking credit course, then reversing the roles by taking a Dale Carnegie course taught by Brock. With his interest in banking now fully engaged, Brock was a quick study and soon became a senior officer of the bank. Not surprisingly, he emerged as the bank's marketing and business development chief. He combined his new banking knowledge with his old instincts for aggressive salesmanship, and people were soon shaking their heads and talking about what Brock had done now.

"Harry Brock was unusual in those days," recalls W. L. "Jack" Hurley, Exchange Security's trust officer who went on to become chairman and CEO of First Alabama Bancshares when Frank Plummer retired. "Bank officers were not aggressive in making sales calls back then, but Harry went out and started drumming up business." Brock, people whispered incredulously at the bank, had even made a cold call on Liberty National Life Insurance Co., one of Birmingham's biggest businesses — just walked in off the sidewalk and said that he wanted to talk to the person who handled their banking business.

Brock probably had more leeway for exercising his talent at Exchange Security than he would have had at either of the city's towering institutions. Exchange Security, the product of a 1957 merger between The Exchange Bank and Security Commercial Bank, was ruled by an old guard, to be sure, but it was a small, homey shop, and a group of talented, hard-working, high-spirited younger men was gaining influence. The old guard was dominated by Sterling Edwards and James Simpson, major shareholders who were technically outside directors but took active roles in the affairs of the bank. Robert Russell was a supportive, somewhat indulgent CEO.

A lot of fire was generated by the young turks, who included Pless, a former bank examiner who had married Edwards' daughter and would go on to become president of the bank, seeing it become part of First Alabama Bancshares before taking an early retirement from banking. There was Brock, who would start Central; Hurley, who would head First Alabama, and Jack Alexander, who would become president and CEO of Colonial Bank. Together they nudged the bank in a more progressive direction and put some new energy into Birmingham banking.

They also had high times together. Hurley recalls fuming at Brock and Pless, who had grabbed an evening's steak off his backyard grill and started playing football with it. "In those days, we didn't have much money, and steak was hard to come by," Hurley explains. On another occasion, at a summer cottage, they tricked Hurley into skinny-dipping, then turned on the spotlights and kept him in the water for quite a while.

"They were intrepid. They'd catch snakes at night. They were high-spirited, a lot of fun, good company," he muses.

Brock's career was solidly on track. His good-natured aggressiveness was winning him some important friends. One of them was James Simpson. An outspoken trial lawyer, a powerful Alabama politician and a dominant director-stockholder of Exchange Security, Simpson was an influential sponsor, and it was apparent to everyone that Simpson liked Brock and encouraged him. "Don't wear white socks in New York, Harry," Simpson once cautioned, teasing Brock about his rural, north Alabama background; but privately, sensing Brock's ambitious nature, he would whisper to Brock that some day he might be running the bank. Brock tried to dismiss such ideas since he was a loyal friend of Norman Pless, the more likely heir apparent, but there was no denying that he was ambitious and that he did want to lead a bank.

Brock also attracted favorable attention from Howard Morris, staff director of the Alabama Bankers Association, who drew Brock into the association's activities and helped to create opportunities for him. Brock won AlaBA's first Outstanding Young Banker Award in 1957 and later served as president of its Young Bankers Section.

Thus Brock became a member in good standing of Alabama's banking fraternity. He was getting the right promotions and the right assignments. Powerful elders had smiled on his enthusiasm. He was building a reputation as a dynamic leader. Jane had not only a washing machine but a dryer, and a nice home to put them in. The good-times kid had discovered drive and direction, then added knowledge and skill without losing his down-to-earth warmth and attractiveness. The world was his oyster. People expected great things of Harry Brock, but no one expected him to embark on a course that would shake the industry to its core and make him fervent enemies as well as admiring friends.

Well, almost no one did. Close friends noticed that Brock was becoming restless and beginning to feel confined by the policies of Exchange Security. With Jane, he openly discussed his frustrations. He knew what to do, he told her, but he wasn't allowed. The only solution, Jane would tell him, the only way to get away from the old men and do what you want, is to start your own bank. Brock would shake his head and say, "One of these days I might. The timing has to be right."

◇

The subject came up again when the morning newspaper reported rumors on June 28 that the Bank for Savings would merge with Birmingham Trust. "As sure as shooting, somebody's going to start a new bank now," Brock observed. "You, maybe?" Jane wondered out loud. Brock just shook his head, she recalls. The timing had to be right. Then Schuyler Baker called, and the timing was suddenly right.

Baker called Daniel back to report his conversation with Brock. "You mean the big red-headed boy over at the Exchange Security? Did you check him out? Do you think he can handle it?" Daniel, who had not met Brock, wanted to know. Baker's answer was affirmative, so it was time for Brock and Daniel to meet.

◇

Central Bank would be built largely by young, ambitious entrepreneurs: hungry people with a stake in the bank and willing, even eager, to work like fanatics to build their own reputations and fortunes as they built the bank. Hugh Daniel did not exactly fit the mold. By 1963, Daniel's reputation and fortune were well established. Daniel Construction Co. was flourishing. It had 1964 assets of $33.3 million, net worth of $17.8 million and net earnings of $2.4 million based on revenue of $129 million. Founded in Greenville, S.C., it was now bicameral, with Hugh Daniel running the Birmingham house while older brother Charlie oversaw operations in Greenville and represented the company nationally. It was a big-time construction company, rapidly becoming international. Daniel, who became chief executive in 1964 when his brother died, was a leading citizen of Birmingham and a man much respected for his business acumen, his personal integrity and his civic leadership. A new bank could hardly have found a more influential backer.

Organizational filings list the organizers' net personal worth: Daniel's was $3.7 million, compared to $520,000 for Frank Hardy, $431,000 for John Israel, $251,000 for Dr. Wendell Taylor, $218,000 for Stewart Welch and $132,000 for Baker.

Personally, Daniel was a quiet man, soft-spoken and inclined to keep his own counsel. He was invariably courteous, almost courtly, in manner. Aggressive competition was deeply ingrained in Daniel, but his style was low-key, and he shied away from publicity, of which Central would produce bumper crops. It was part of his credo as a businessman that friends are important, that you are loyal to your friends, and that you help people who help you.

He hardly needed a bank. Daniel Construction Co. and Daniel personally would have been prime customers for any bank. He had already made his mark and reserved his place in history. But he believed Birmingham needed a new bank. He came from a world where construction workers got paid on Fridays and often couldn't get to a bank until Saturday morning to get their money for the weekend and the following week. Banks were supposed to serve the public, and the part of the public Daniel knew best needed to bank on Saturdays. He made sure that his bank, the Bank for Savings, was open on Saturdays. Now the Bank for Savings was disappearing into Birmingham Trust, and BTNB was a no-Saturday-hours bank. Saturday banking was about to vanish, and this irritated Daniel.

Daniel took a real interest in banking. He had been a hard-working director at the Bank of Savings, using his influence to bring business to that bank. Legend has it that Daniel was out soliciting business for the Bank of Savings on the day when the other directors, without his knowledge, were negotiating to sell it. It was no secret that he opposed the sale and was miffed when the deal went forward.

◇

When Brock called on Daniel, he found the builder to be a ready investor, prepared to take "all or any part of" the new bank's capital stock. The new bank should be capitalized at $1 million, Brock explained, and he wanted Daniel, along with the other organizers, to sign a note to borrow the $1 million to temporarily finance the stock, which would then be resold at the same price (500,000 shares at $2 apiece) to a broad base of Alabama investors whom Brock would pick. That arrangement suited Daniel fine. He mentioned the Saturday hours, and Brock agreed.

But Brock would have to sell Daniel on getting involved in the new bank. He couldn't take an active role in the affairs of the bank, Daniel explained, and he declined to go on its board, citing his directorship of the still-existent Bank for Savings.

There was one other thing, Daniel added. If there were no other strong New York ties, could the new bank do its correspondent business with Chemical Bank? Chemical was a Daniel Construction Co. bank and brother Charlie was a member of its board. Brock grinned. He was not at all sorry to see that Daniel sought to solicit a little business for a bank he cared about.

◇

Most of Brock's colleagues at Exchange Security Bank were stunned by his decision to leave and start a new bank, and more than a few thought he was crazy. In retrospect, it is clear that 1963 witnessed a great wave of new bank formations. James Saxon, as Comptroller of the Currency, was shaking up the industry by encouraging the chartering of new national banks, and many state banking departments were following suit. There were 312 new banks opened in 1964, 11 of them in Alabama. Well over a thousand new banks would be started in the mid '60s, and many of them would be quite successful, though none more so than Central. This trend was not apparent, however, to either Brock or those who questioned his sanity. There had been no successful start-up in Birmingham since 1944.

The local economy, still dominated by steel, was vulnerable to strikes and recessions, and economic growth in Jefferson County was sluggish at best. On top of that, the racial unrest was making everyone wary. Confidence was in short supply. Brock calls it "Birmingham's darkest hour."

That a popular, successful banker would leave a prestigious senior officer position at an established, profitable bank and stake his future and that of his family on the success of a new venture seemed like a reckless gamble. A few wondered out loud if Brock, after only eight years of banking experience, mostly in the marketing and business development end, was a complete enough banker to steer a new bank. Some who had invested in Brock's training thought his switch smacked of ingratitude. Brock's leaving particularly strained his relations with Simpson.

The resentment at Exchange Security only got worse when Brock began hiring key officers and employees of that bank to work for Central, then started picking off some of the key accounts of his old bank.

Brock was not just selling his time to this untested enterprise; he was putting as much of his own money into it as he could. He withdrew his profit-sharing balance from Exchange Security to invest it in Central stock, Hurley recalls.

So Brock gave his old employer 60 days notice and closed one eventful chapter in his career. The new bank had a kind of paper existence at this point. The names on the paper were Baker's, Stewart Welch's, Dr. Wendell Taylor's, John Israel's and Frank Hardy's. Brock's name went on the paper on New Year's Eve. A change in the federal tax law would place restrictions on stock options for employees hired after December 31, 1963, and stock options were a key part of the deal between Central and Brock. It was important to beat the deadline, so what would soon be known around Birmingham as "the Central crowd" had an official New Year's Eve party at the Daniel Construction Co. offices at 4 p.m. as 1964 rolled into sight. Baker presided at this first official board meeting. Daniel by this time had been persuaded to join the board. He was duly elected and then invited to join the meeting. Then Brock was hired as "general manager" at a salary of $25,000, and the stock option contract was executed, giving him a ten-year option at $2 a share on 50,000 shares of Central stock. An auspicious new year was toasted in.

CHAPTER TWO

Getting Ready

AT THE THIRD BOARD meeting, on January 10, 1964, Baker resigned as president, and Brock advanced from general manager to president and chief executive. The board operated without a chairman until Daniel was persuaded to take the position on February 27, two days before Central Bank opened its doors. In those hectic first two months of 1964, an idea had to be turned into a bank — a vital, functioning business with a staff, a building, capital and customers.

Recruiting a staff was crucial. Brock knew who the bank's second officer should be. He had his eye on Lloyd Rains, an assistant vice president at Exchange Security and a friend from his auto-selling days in Gadsden. Rains was a credit man. He had learned to size up a good loan by financing automobiles. He switched to bank lending in 1960 when Brock introduced him to Pless and helped him get a job at Exchange Security. At the bank, Rains made installment loans, then commercial loans.

A cautious lender and a soft-spoken, even-tempered man, Rains was a good foil to the more mercurial Brock. The two men would work well together as a team and lead Central through its formative years. Rains was cautious enough that Brock had to do some convincing. How big would the new bank be in four or five years, Rains wanted to know. "Oh, $8 or $10 million," Brock replied. That satisfied Rains, who signed on and went to work.

Actually, Brock gave Rains a lower estimate than the headier version the organizers put down on a *pro forma* projection they filed with the regulators. There they anticipated an $11 million bank after only three years. Since there were no recent start-ups to go by, a realistic growth estimate was hard to make.

The bank had no building yet, so Brock and Rains rolled up their sleeves and worked through January 1964 in the library at Baker's law firm, Baker, McDaniel and Hall. They made lists. They filled up yellow tablets with names of prospects. The first order of business was to capitalize the new bank — to finish placing the $1 million of initial stock, but Brock was already looking past the first order of business to the second and maybe even the third. He was more than ever determined to build business at the same time he sold stock, to make sure the stock went only to people who would do business with the bank.

Baker proved particularly adept at drumming up investor interest. Taylor, Welch and Hardy were also spreading the word among their friends and associates. Brock and Rains were getting lots of calls from people who wanted stock. They had a hit on their hands. A new bank in Birmingham, perhaps benefiting from Daniel's association with it, was, in Rains' words, "unusual, exciting, glamorous." They were quickly becoming oversubscribed. Brock announced at the January 26 board meeting that 247,650 shares had been placed. Less than two weeks later, he was explaining that orders exceeded available stock.

Baker had been a bit too generous in promising his lawyer friends 5,000-share lots, Brock and Rains decided. It was time to unsell some stock. Brock and Rains got on the phones. It looks like we won't be able to sell you 5,000 shares, they would explain. There's not much available, and we're going to have to pro-rate it according to how much money people deposit with us. How much would you like to keep on deposit?

The prospect lists were searched again, with an eye to how much business each one could bring to the bank, and names were transferred to file cards. Those who weren't potential customers went into a reject pile. Somewhere in this winnowing process the Ten-for-One Club was born. In retrospect, it was vintage Central Bank marketing. Prospects would be invited to buy stock and to put ten times the value of the stock on deposit when the bank opened. If you wanted 5,000 shares at $2 a share, fine. You could keep $100,000 in a checking account. Small investors wanting only 100 shares could get them with no strings attached, but larger investors were urged to come up with a ten-times-greater deposit. If they did, they got their stock and their pin: their Ten-for-One pin, designed by Dr. Taylor, using the Central logo, and ordered by Rains from the Balfour Company. The club held breakfast meetings twice a month.

"It worked," says Rains with a grin. People would come into the bank or approach a Central banker and ask how they could get one of the pins, how they could join the Ten-for-One Club. The deposit pledges were gentlemen's agreements, but only three of the 5,000-share investors failed to come through with the promised deposits, as Rains recalls it. Central had turned its investors into its best customers, then organized them into a booster club. By February 29, Brock told the board, the stock had been distributed among 565 subscribers, each of whom had signed a pledge to do business with the new bank.

Daniel was by now an active member of the Central team, and a healthy number of Daniel Construction Co. employees and subcontractors were among the original investor-depositors. One of Daniel's calls went to his son, Bill, who was working in Greenville at the time.

"It looks like we're going to go ahead with the new bank," Bill remembers his father saying. "I'll hold some stock for you if you'd like. Of course, this thing could be a disaster. If you put your money in, it might be ten years before you could get it back out." Bill took a chance on 5,000 shares.

Central was not issuing stock in January — just taking orders, filling up legal pads and file cards with handwritten notations of who was to get how much and what they had pledged to deposit. To issue the stock, Central needed a bank which would temporarily finance the offering with a $1 million loan and act as transfer agent, issuing the stock as payment was received.

Brock's idea of a sharp banker was Mills B. Lane, the dynamic, aggressive head of the C&S National Bank of Atlanta. So when Brock took a day off from his activities in Birmingham to go to Atlanta to borrow the interim funding, he followed his sentiments to C&S. Lane was out of the bank that day, but a senior lending officer listened to what Brock was planning to do. He wasn't sold. "Birmingham doesn't need another bank," Brock was told. "It has too many already." Loan denied.

He went across the street to the First National Bank of Atlanta and talked to another high-ranking loan officer. He was turned down again. Brock knew that Birmingham was not considered the land of opportunity, especially in Atlanta, but he hadn't expected this much trouble, not with Hugh Daniel ready to sign the note. The big Atlanta banks must be protecting their relationships with the big Birmingham banks, he decided.

He was crossing Marietta Street on his way to Fulton National Bank and a possible third strikeout when he decided to call Frank Morast instead. Morast was president of Hamilton National Bank in Chattanooga and, as a correspondent officer, had called on Brock at Exchange Security. Brock thought a lot of him. So he veered off to a sidewalk pay phone and called Chattanooga. Morast was out of his office; could he return Brock's call? Brock watched the traffic move by. No, he said, that was all right; he'd call again in the morning.

When he reached Morast the next day, Morast took the information, checked it out with his people and quickly got back to Brock. Green light. Brock had found his banker. Hamilton would advance the $1 million and take care of issuing the stock.

The new bank did have a name. That had already been chosen by January 1964. Lots of possibilities had been discussed, some of them by Brock and Red Leach as they sat on Leach's living room floor and watched their children play nearby. Brock finally picked Central because the letter C was a good logo letter, graphically adaptable, attractive on pencils, matchbooks, and billboards, he recalls. Because there were strong Central Banks in other states, he figured he might pick up a little business from people moving to Birmingham from those states. Later, in his marketing gospel, he would tell his staff that the C also stood for customer. He seemed unaware that the name might presage the center of a statewide banking system.

The new bank needed a home. The frenetic activity was getting in the way of Baker's law practice, and Central would of course need a good streetfront location when it opened its doors to the public. There were plenty of vacant buildings in downtown Birmingham then. The best site seemed to be the old City Federal Savings & Loan building on First Avenue between 20th and 21st Streets, a four-story structure with a first floor already laid out for a financial institution. With Daniel's help, the building was bought for $145,000, and $22,000 was allocated for renovations and fixtures. Brock, Rains and their growing crew moved into the new quarters in February, with renovation still underway downstairs.

The bank's first address was an easy-to-find location. It made Central practically a next-door neighbor to the mighty First National of Birmingham, giving rise to the tongue-in-cheek claim that upstart Central was "next to the largest bank in Alabama."

The Central team was rapidly being assembled. Early on, Brock had hired away from Exchange Security his former secretary, Frances Anderson. Floyd Jones, who had been an assistant vice president at the old Bank for Savings, was hired as cashier. Young Frances Guthrie, identified by Rains as "one of the fastest proof operators in the state of Alabama," left Exchange Security to become the foundation of the new bank's operations department. By opening day, there were 11 employees. There was such a strong sense of glamour and adventure about the new enterprise that it was not hard to recruit a good staff. Brock and Rains drew heavily on known quantities from Exchange Security in building the initial staff. Though Brock was accused of "raiding" his old bank, he insists that he recruited only Rains — that the others all came and asked to work for Central.

As opening day approached, the work pace became even more intense. Checks for stock purchases were sought and sent along to the Hamilton in Chattanooga. Prospective customers were asked to stop by to order their new checks and sign signature cards for their checking accounts. Active solicitation of business continued without letup. Prospects had been translated from scratch pads to three-by-five file cards, Rains recalls, and divided into three piles: good prospects on salmon-colored cards, fair ones, and rejects on yellow or white cards. It was the beginning of a long habit of collecting and listing pertinent data and organizing it on cards. Central would embrace computers in a timely fashion, but would remain a big user of file cards.

Late hours, high spirits and stacks of file cards were hallmarks of the new bank as it prepared to open its doors. Days started with 6 a.m. breakfast meetings and frequently ended at midnight — when it was finally too late to make one more call. "We were having a great time," Rains recalls.

Finally, it was time. Brock put in one more long day on Sunday, March 1, showing out the local TV crew at the end of a half-hour telecast paid for by the bank to publicize its next-day opening. It was time for the final pep rally before the big game, the dinner party for Central's 11 employees and their spouses. Brock had a foretaste of his new responsibilities when his young son, Buck, after hearing about plans for the dinner, asked, "Do you mean Dad's going to be responsible for feeding 22 people?"

He took one last look at the premises. The remodeling finished, the first floor looked sharp. A balcony office for private conferences was well appointed. The row of desks in the lobby — Anderson's, then Rains', then Brock's — were tidy, file cards safely out of view. Upstairs, the operations area was nearly empty, save for Guthrie's proof machine, but that was room to grow in. They were ready, Brock decided, and flipped out the lights and went on to dinner.

CHAPTER THREE

Hitting The Streets

THE SUN DID NOT SHINE on Central Bank and Trust Company's first day in business. Birmingham woke up on March 2, 1964, to the sound of raindrops on rooftops and cars sloshing along wet streets. It would be an all-day rain.

On hand to help open the new bank was Governor George Wallace. The governor didn't normally attend bank openings, but Baker was a friend and important political supporter, so he made the trip from Montgomery to Birmingham to take part in the festivities. His presence brought a number of people through the rain and into the bank, including one group the Central people had never expected to see.

The president of the First National Bank of Birmingham was John Hand, for whom the John Hand Building is named. Hand was a tough, autocratic banker of the old school and well aware of his importance. When the governor of the state and the state's leading banker are but a few dozen yards apart, good sense and good manners dictate that they meet, Hand thought. So he called Central, asked for the governor, and invited him to stop by First National.

The governor would be delighted to see Mr. Hand, he learned, but was in town as Central Bank's guest and was involved in the opening activities at Central. Wouldn't Mr. Hand come there to see him? So John Hand, with a small entourage of senior officers in tow, walked outside, up the wet sidewalk and into Central Bank to see the governor.

A little later, Wallace decided that he wanted to meet the back-office employees and asked to be taken upstairs. Baker was reluctant, but Wallace insisted, so upstairs they went. There, in a large, nearly empty room, the governor discovered

Frances Guthrie, all alone, doing some clerical work. "What are you running here, Schuyler, a con game?" Wallace joked, as Baker recalls.

By the time they closed the doors in the afternoon, Central had taken in $3.7 million in deposits. "If we had made one more trip to the post office and counted the checks in the final mail, we would have made it to $4 million," Rains recalls. It was, a quick check indicated, the most a new Alabama bank had ever taken in on its first day.

The money was not primarily walk-in business, of course. Central had set itself up for a fast start by soliciting deposits in advance and linking stock sales to deposit pledges. Indeed, Brock had told directors at the February 29 board meeting that commitments for first-day deposits exceeded $4 million. If the numbers on the file cards and adding machine tapes held up, there was $12 million worth of promised checking account deposits to expect over the next several months. By the end of the first six weeks Central reported $5.9 million in deposits.

Loan growth, Brock warned, would take longer. Central laid off the bulk of its opening deposits ($3 million) in U.S. Treasury notes at 3.87 percent, bought $300,000 of automobile loans from the Alabama Farm Bureau and signaled its correspondents (Hamilton in Chattanooga and Chemical in New York) that it was interested in participations in quality secured loans.

With little real growth in the Birmingham economy, Central, if it was to grow rapidly, would have to take customers away from the other banks in town. Building a large bank is normally a glacial process: adding a new arrival to the community here, picking up another bank's dissatisfied loan reject there, and slowly making them add up. Just as the two banks started in the 1920s were dwarfed by the two banks started in the 1800s, Central was likely to remain forever overshadowed by all of the mainstream Birmingham banks unless its people did something really startling. Brock thought he saw an opening or two — a few bold ways to capitalize on Central's strengths and his competitors' weaknesses.

He set out to build a selling organization. His competitors, he was sure, didn't know beans about selling, didn't even think they needed to. "Banking in those days was not just conservative; it was feudal," Hurley, CEO of First Alabama, recalls of Birmingham in the 1960s. Banks accepted deposits. People filed loan supplications and banks occasionally granted them, on their own terms. It was unusual for a banker to go out from the marble halls into the street and actually ask for business. Customers went to banks; banks did not go to customers.

Brock had had a taste of selling banking services at Exchange Security. Now he would build an entire bank around it, instilling a sales philosophy in the whole Central organization. He would field the only bank in town that was completely, aggressively dedicated to selling banking.

And his elite commando corps would be his directors. It was a radical idea, expecting directors to go out and make sales calls. Most bank presidents approached their boards deferentially, even reverentially, as stewards accounting to their masters. Brock approached his board like Vince Lombardi addressing the Green Bay Packers. He set out to raise their competitive spirits, to build their desire to win.

It was considered audacious in most banks to try to dictate where directors would do their own banking, although they were expected to favor the bank they directed. At Central it was a point of faith that every director did all of his own banking, and that of businesses he controlled, with Central. Brock considered it loyalty to the cause.

But it went further than that. Directors, chosen because of their extensive business ties and the amount of banking business they could influence, were expected to fully exert that influence, to evangelize among their personal and business acquaintances, to take time from their jobs to go out and regularly make sales calls for Central.

And it worked. It worked partly because the original directors were a close-knit, high-spirited group; because they were not just directors but founders; because they had invested heavily in Central stock and would benefit directly from its prospering; because most of them were young and ambitious and still out to make their mark on the world; and because they had a forceful salesman egging them on, cheering them, congratulating them, challenging them, showing them how. It was almost a grand game. Strangely, most of them discovered that it was fun.

On a typical day, Brock would call Daniel, pick him up, and the two of them would call on an important local businessman. Daniel would get the door open, and Brock would make the pitch. The businessman would be amazed; he'd probably never had a banker call on him, in his own place of business, before. He was flattered that Hugh Daniel had come to see him, and he found Brock to be mighty persuasive. Often he would decide to bank with Central.

Other directors were also successful at bringing in business. As an orthodontist, Taylor would shut down his practice for an afternoon to go out soliciting business for Central and would spend his days off making sales calls. When a new branch was about to open, Taylor would go to the neighborhood and start working the streets. "People would just be astounded that a director was out knocking on doors, soliciting business," Taylor recalls. "We got a lot of business that way."

As Stewart Welch remembers it, "Harry did a good job of motivating us, selling us on building the bank. He used Dale Carnegie techniques and kept records. We'd team up and go up and down the streets, calling on businesses. It was fun to call on people who were not used to being called on by a banker. Mostly bankers never left the four walls of the bank."

By the time others were invited to join the board, the sales culture was firmly established. Newcomers were absorbed into a small band of dedicated promoters. Actively working to sell the bank was a stipulation for board membership, Brock recalls explaining to prospective directors. Once in a while, he found himself (usually temporarily) with a director who wouldn't sell, but most of the time they got religion. It was probably equally true that Central only went for directors who would be willing and able to sell the bank and had the contacts and leverage to direct a lot of valuable business to the bank when they did try.

Central started with the smallest board in Birmingham and, with the exception of Hugh Daniel, probably the least prestigious, but in short order it became the most productive.

No other board in town could come close to bringing in business like "the Central crowd."

As Brock remembers it, he knew from his first conversation with Baker that Central must have a committed, hard-working, sales-oriented board. All that followed was carrying out that plan. As most of the early directors recall it, the concept of the selling board evolved from the intensity of the first months of trying to establish the new bank and the rather heady success they enjoyed.

By all accounts, the effort was a huge success. At the suggestion of John Evins, a home appliance distributor who joined the board in March 1965 and became one of Central's legendary salesmen, Brock went from keeping records to sponsoring sales contests. Trips were awarded to directors who brought in the most new business. Contests were kicked off with festive dinners at which wives were shrewdly included and informed about the prizes their husbands might win. Individuals bet each other steak dinners in the spirit of friendly rivalry. The biggest producers, often Evins, Daniel, and J. Wallace Nall, who joined the board in May 1965, were showered with gifts and accolades. Nonproducers suffered in embarrassed silence when reports were read aloud in board meetings, indicating who had brought in how much new business.

By the early 1970s, Central probably had the best board in the nation for producing business, and had become famous for it. It had been enlarged in 1970 to include Inos Heard, Thomas E. Jernigan, Marshall Durbin, Jr., and Ben F. Harrison. Banks around the country inquired about Central's program, then tried to imitate it. Productive directors such as Carl Wittichen, elected to the State National board in 1970, then moved to the Central Bank of Birmingham board in 1973, were brought in by other banks to speak to their boards. Few of the other banks had great success. They didn't start from the very beginning with selling directors, and they didn't have Harry Brock, insiders at Central would point out knowingly.

Such aggressive pursuit of business by directors was not universally admired in Birmingham. Howls went up from the other banks in town that Central was resorting to hard-ball tactics and unfairly compelling some reluctant converts onto its customer lists. Such complaints usually centered on Daniel. Daniel Construction Co. did business with many suppliers and subcontractors. Rival bankers still tell stories of long-time customers coming to explain that they were moving their accounts to Central, that they didn't want to change banks, but that Hugh Daniel had spread the word that he wanted them to and they didn't dare get crossed up with Hugh Daniel. At Central, Daniel was hailed as "helpful" and "influential"; in other banks he was called "powerful."

As founding director Frank Hardy explains the process, directors were chosen for their contacts in different segments of Birmingham's business. As a heating, plumbing and air conditioning contractor, Hardy covered a blue-collar beat. He contacted his friends, colleagues and suppliers and asked them to bank with Central. "We got a lot of good accounts that way, but we also got a lot of token accounts," Hardy explains. When information came back from the bank identifying the token accounts, Hardy "would have to go back after them again."

Admirers and detractors alike agreed on one thing: that Central was doing one hell of an aggressive, industrious and effective job of "asking for the business." "Ask for the business," the perennial motto of the salesman, was permeating the organization. Director John Israel remembers once stopping to see a business associate briefly while his wife waited in the car. When he returned to the car, she asked him, "Well, did you ask for the business for Central?"

Later, when Carolyn Robertson, longtime aide to Brock, joined the staff, she would report a social encounter with a "Guess who I saw last night" story. Brock would listen, then come back with the inevitable response: "Did you ask for the business?" "Eventually it just gets in your system," Robertson reports. "I do it all the time now without even thinking about it."

The bank's small, mostly young staff didn't all have the same leverage or opportunities to bring in new business as the directors did, but they were just as fired up and eager to build the bank. The early employees of the bank, whether they stayed with Central or went on to other employers, whether they later clashed with Central policies or got along well with them, all remember their work at the bank in 1964-67 as wonderful, exhilarating days, marked by hard work, high spirits and a feeling that, against long odds, they were winning.

"It was a ball. Everybody did what it took to get the job done and had a good time. Some of the happiest days of my life were spent at Central Bank," recalls Jim Lovell, who later left to help start a rival bank and then formed his own insurance agency. "People just worked like hell and loved it. When you're successful, it makes all the difference. In the early years, it seemed like we always won. I can't remember losing. It was a ton of fun."

Lovell recalls that when the bank closed its doors at noon on Saturdays, employees would hang around to plan and talk about banking, then go over to "Andy's" for sandwiches and more bank talk, often waiting until evening to go home. They didn't want to stop. Brock used to tell them to go home and see their wives now and then.

"We didn't know what five o'clock was," recalls Frances Guthrie, who stayed with Central to become vice president for operations. We rarely quit before seven, but we didn't mind. We were all so excited about the opportunity and so committed to making a go of it that we didn't even think about the time."

Guthrie, like most of the staff, had left a secure job at Exchange Security and had endured the grim warnings of co-workers: "You'll be out of business in no time and begging to have your old job back." But they *were* making a go of it and then some. They were winning — and more than ever getting the cold shoulder from some of their Exchange Security colleagues, Guthrie recalls.

As the bank prospered and grew, the work load mounted. Everyone would pitch in to get the big jobs done. "When it came to statement time, Mr. Brock and Mr. Rains would be wrapping statements just like the rest of us," reports Guthrie, and sometimes Baker would drop by and be recruited to stuff statements too. Brock would sometimes run the postage meter, she adds.

Brock, particularly, seemed endowed with boundless energy. He would be at the front door every morning for the first several months to greet each employee as he or she arrived, and he would not leave the bank at night as long as anyone was still working, but would help until the job was done, Guthrie recalls. The young bank was so eager for deposits in those days, recalls Garry Smith, a Daniel Construction Co. officer, that you could call the bank if you had a check for deposit and they'd send someone right over to pick it up.

The personal anxiety, the skepticism of the outside world, the long hours, the camaraderie, the sense of "us against the giants," and finally the thrill of victory created an emotional crucible which left its mark on everyone who went through it. It created a strong sense of loyalty, loyalty to each other but also to the cause, and the cause was Central Bank. To this cause, personal sacrifices were expected and gladly offered. It gave rise to a strong loyalty ethic that would remain stamped on Central Bank. In the name of loyalty, much was tolerated on all sides. Outsiders often perceived Central as brash, tough and mercenary, but insiders understood very well its sentimental core.

From the very beginning, Central Bank courted publicity. Brock personally liked limelight, and he thought that it would help the bank to call attention to what Central was doing. So he set out not only to overthrow a lot of old Birmingham banking traditions but to publicly call attention to these actions, a fact which added to the irritation the old guard felt toward the abrasive newcomer. True to its original purpose, Central, from the beginning, opened on Saturdays and advertised Saturday banking in its first newspaper ads. Saturday banking, by one account, prompted a visit by John Hand and a couple of his minions to Birmingham Trust, where they paid a courtesy call on Will Cothran, who had succeeded Frank Plummer as BTNB's president. They informed Cothran, as a professional courtesy, that First National would soon begin Saturday openings. Cothran called in his retail banking chief, Guy Caffee, to discuss Saturday banking. Caffee pointed out that it would be unpopular among his staff, then added that it would be particularly annoying to watch Harry Brock on Channel 13 telling how he made the big banks open on Saturday. That does it, Hand is supposed to have said as he turned on his heel. First National would not open on Saturdays. And it didn't.

There was more to the new bank's business plan than simply high-powered selling. Even the best of salesmen must have products to sell. Once Central had digested the first wave of new account openings and business had settled into something resembling a routine, it was time to pursue certain types of business where Central could outshine its competitors: ideally, lines where Central could make a good profit and enjoy rapid growth. It found one in correspondent banking.

Correspondent banks were bankers' banks, wholesale operations in which a strong "upstream" bank rendered certain services to its "downstream" respondents in return for compensating balances, free deposits placed in the upstream bank. In a principal correspondent relationship, the balances could be substantial. Theoretically, if a bank could gear up to offer valuable services to downstream banks and then sign up enough customers, it could build a large base of free deposits — a source of growth and profit.

But correspondent banks were usually large banks selling excess capacity to small banks. Central was the size of a typical downstream bank. It could not sell the expertise of a large, diverse, sophisticated staff — lawyers, bond traders, trust officers, and so forth. It lacked even a trust department. It did not have a large legal lending limit, so it couldn't help downstream banks make oversized loans. It had no Federal Reserve System membership to offer. It had no data processing department. It lacked many of the basic tools of the correspondent banking trade.

Central was unfazed by these obstacles. If it couldn't offer a full range of correspondent services, it would specialize in a few essential ones that it could render well. Correspondent banks were and are essential links in the payment system because small banks count on correspondents to clear their checks. They would keep those checks written by their own customers and perhaps exchange locally those drawn on other nearby banks. The rest would be sent off to a correspondent for clearing and settlement.

In 1964, there were still non-par banks, banks that did not

pay out the full face value (par value) of checks drawn on themselves but kept back a small amount (normally one-eighth of 1 percent) for the bank, almost as a service charge. An $80 check drawn on a non-par bank might actually be worth only $79.90. Non-par checks were unpopular in powerful places by 1964 and were marked for extinction. Regulators and large banks considered them a nuisance. The Fed refused to process non-par checks, which meant that all of its members — all national banks and some state banks — were par banks. It also meant that non-par banks could not use the Fed but had to clear their checks through correspondents. Non-par checks were an emotional issue among many of the small state-chartered banks, which fought vigorously until the end to preserve their right to take off a small payment.

By 1971, every state in the South except Louisiana had passed laws banning non-par checks, but in 1964 there were still a lot of non-par banks in Alabama, Georgia, Tennessee, Mississippi, South Carolina and Louisiana. With all those $79.90 checks moving around the South, someone had to come up with the missing dimes. It didn't make sense to most correspondent banks that they should do so; they were middlemen. But Central Bank saw an opportunity to buy a lot of .125-percent tickets into the correspondent ballgame. Central would throw in the nickels and dimes and clear all checks at par. It gave Central a pricing edge in the marketplace.

Central also saw a need among small banks for good audit and investment services, so it assembled strong departments in these areas so that it could sell such services to correspondents.

Quality services at competitive prices, the keys to most business success, were probably what made Central succeed in correspondent banking, especially when such services were aggressively sold. But Central went a couple of steps further. It knew that most small banks did business with whomever the CEO wanted to do business with, so it took steps to appeal to the CEOs. Many country bank presidents were also major shareholders in their banks, and some of them had much of their wealth tied up in bank stock. Country bank stock was not liquid. And because it didn't trade frequently, its market value was difficult to appraise. Few upstream correspondents were willing to make loans collateralized by bank stock for their respondents. Central was happy to make them and, in the process, cemented many correspondent relationships.

Central also made sure its correspondent customers enjoyed the business relationship. Even the non-selling banks found it expedient to do a bit of wining and dining of correspondent customers. Central introduced new levels of wining and dining. "It was the highlight of many a banker's year to get invited to a Central Bank party," recalls Lovell, who was part of Central's correspondent operation from 1966-74. "When we had a party, we did it right. We were known as a first-class operation. We didn't worry about spending a penny here or there if it pleased the customer and made him like Central Bank. It was part of our being customer oriented. We had a good time and made good money."

Central took busloads of country bankers to Alabama and Auburn football games. Perhaps the ultimate experiences offered to correspondent customers were the week-long seminars Central sponsored annually. For many years the seminars were held in some of the most elegant places in the world. Good banking information was always provided, but so were good times. Friendships flourished in the seminar environment. "There was a fraternity sort of feeling," notes Carlton "Pinky" Pinkerton, who headed the correspondent department for many years. "It was an ideal climate for developing relationships."

Central entered correspondent banking early. Brock discussed it at the August 10, 1964, board meeting, then reported four accounts and $140,000 in balances at the September 14 meeting. By October 12, 11 banks had more than $1 million on deposit at Central.

A lot of the rapid growth of Central's correspondent business was due to the efforts of Clyde Tate. Tate had not come from Exchange Security — or from any bank. He came in the summer of 1964 from the treasurer's office of the U.S. Steel plant in Birmingham. He handled funds there, thought he could become a banker and asked Brock for a job.

Tate's first assignment was to build Central into a correspondent power. If the bank's directors hit the streets, Tate hit the road, traveling throughout Alabama, then Georgia, then Tennessee and Florida, asking for the business. He was, Rains says, "along with Harry Brock, the best salesman that ever was — anywhere."

Pinkerton, who came from Exchange Security, became Central's second correspondent banker, assigned to spread the business to Georgia. Pinkerton recalls working Georgia for the first six months of 1966 without getting a single account, then signing up four in his seventh month. After six more months, there were 21. After two years, there were 103. Eventually there would be 160 in Georgia alone, Pinkerton says, making Central one of the leading correspondent banks in that state.

Tennessee became fruitful territory as well. For several years, Central had more than 100 bank customers in each of Alabama, Georgia and Tennessee, with fewer in Mississippi, Florida, Louisiana and Kentucky. "At one point, 30 percent of the bank's deposits were in correspondent balances," Pinkerton recalls. Correspondent balances accounted for more than 20 percent of total deposits through much of 1965 and 1966.

An equally controversial but probably less important source of Central's successful growth was its solicitation of state funds. The state government, at various times of the year, was a large depositor that spread its funds more or less evenhandedly among banks in the state. State deposits during Central's early years did not earn interest, so they were a quite profitable if somewhat unstable source of funds.

Rumors flourished that Central got more than its share. Gossips claimed that the bank should have been called the "George C. Wallace Trust Co." Rivals sniffed that state funds were procured by "playing footsie with the politicians." It was the beginning of Central's reputation for being politically savvy, a resource that would later be put to the test.

Lloyd Rains concedes that the bank got a generous share of state money but says that it did so by applying the same diligent "asking for the business" approach that it used with Birmingham businessmen. "We were accused of receiving political favors. But all we did was pay attention, find out who the key people were, do our homework and make our calls," according to Rains. "Anybody smart would try to get those deposits." He points out that Central helped to change the system so that the state earned interest on its deposits.

Before the doors had even opened, Brock got approval to buy $10,000 worth of state bonds which could be pledged to get state deposits. Call reports show Central with $3.2 million in state deposits at the end of 1964 (23 percent of total deposits), $6.3 million at the end of 1965 (20.6 percent), $9 million at year-end 1966 (18 percent) and $13.7 million at year-end 1967 (20.2 percent), but actual state deposit levels between reporting periods were sometimes higher.

Brock attributes much of the carping about Central's large state deposits to a single $25 million bond issue Central managed for the state in 1965. Banks which served as paying agent or trustee on a state bond issue could not receive fees for their efforts and historically were remunerated with deposits instead, Brock explains. That 1965 bond issue, which was awarded to Central during the first Wallace administration, was the subject of a critical news story in the Birmingham *News,* a "hatchet job," according to Brock, that failed to point out that the deposits were compensation for paying agency activities and were paid out in the ordinary course of business during the next seven days.

Deposits of state agencies and departments are placed by the state treasurer, not the governor, Brock notes, and here he explains Central's success in a different way. The state treasurer in Central's early days was Mary Texas Garner, who was the kid sister of John Frank Hunt, Brock's high school roommate at Tennessee Military Institute in Sweetwater. Brock had made a $25 contribution to her campaign when she ran for secretary of state, he recalls, and received a nice note thanking him. When she was later elected state treasurer, he called on her, was greeted warmly, and when the conversation turned to state deposits, she asked him, "How much do you want?"

"Well, I really shouldn't take any more than the government bonds we own," Brock replied.

"Then how much can you take?" she wanted to know. Brock walked away with the largest amount he could accept, based on the bonds he could put up as surety. "When we were kids, you were the only one of my brother's friends who was nice to me," she confided before he left.

"Based on our size, we did well. We did very well," Brock says unapologetically about Central's state deposits. But after the Birmingham *News* article, he was sensitive enough to rumors about Central's political connections to make a rare request of John Hand one day. It was time for banks to publish financial information in local newspapers, and Brock preferred to list fewer state deposits. He asked Hand if he could temporarily lay some state money off with First National. Hand indignantly refused. Brock conveyed the problem to the state treasurer, who called Hand, and as a favor to the treasurer, Hand allowed the deposits to make a brief visit to First National.

Central recognized the importance of the treasurer's good will enough to hold an early dinner party in her honor, according to the board minutes for February 27, 1964. Central would fête many of its friends and employees, but among the first it chose to honor were Mary Texas Garner and Frank Morast, its sponsor from Hamilton National.

Central's initial business strategy paid off handsomely in the influx of deposits, many of which required service but no interest payments. Loans were another story. The first day's figures, for example, recorded $3.7 million in deposits but only $212,480 in loans. Central's state deposits and correspondent balances, added to its aggressive business solicitation in the Birmingham area, made it liability rich. Until its loan portfolio had time to grow, the excess deposits were invested, first through the Hamilton National Bank in Chattanooga and then, as Central built its own strong investment department, by its own people.

Lending is typically the hardest suit for a new bank to master. The easiest way to grow rapidly is to make loans to people your competitors have turned down. You can charge high rates, the customers come looking for you, and wishful thinking can easily convince even seasoned bankers that a borderline credit risk is really a reasonable loan to make. It's tough to turn away customers when you're struggling to get started yourself.

Central avoided the credit pitfalls that damage many aggressive new banks. It made very few bad loans, especially in the early years. Its rapid growth was facilitated by capital from retained earnings, money that was not drained away in loan write-offs. "You wouldn't believe the loan applications that came in," Rains recalls. "People crawled out from under every rock in the territory to come to us for loans. We turned down a lot of loans, but we tried to do it as nicely as we could so as not to alienate the customer."

Rains and Brock worked out a system. "If Harry said, 'I want you to make this loan,' I made it. If he said, 'I want you to check this out,' I knew I was on my own, free to make my own decision." It was a duet. Brock sang the friendly, accommodating marketing melody, then Rains came in with the sobering low notes of tough credit standards. Both men wanted to keep credit standards high, but it fell to Rains, with his finance company background, to guard the door. He did his job well. In 1964, Central charged off only two loans for $337.42 and $108.06 worth of overdrafts for a total loss of $445.48, less than .007 percent of loans. By the end of 1966, after nearly three years of operation, it had charged off less than $4,000 in loans. It helped that the other banks in Birmingham also held to high credit standards.

Central did find some fruitful areas for building good loan business. It identified and began to serve market segments the other banks had ignored. No other bank in town offered financing secured by inventory or accounts receivable, so Central did. The loans were not prestigious, but Rains knew how to make them and monitor them, and the bank worked well with the merchants and contractors who came to them. "It was a real satisfaction to work with someone who was struggling and see him improve until he got completely out of debt," Rains remembers. There were a few close calls but no losses from such loans. A couple of the borrowers went under, but the liquidation provided enough to pay back the bank. Far more customers went on to prosper and become unsecured borrowers.

Central found another natural rapport with people starting up new businesses and with professional managers wanting to buy out their employers. "A lot of these people had actually been running the businesses for years and knew exactly how things should be done, but they didn't have the net worth to qualify them for loans at other banks," Brock explains. "We made a lot of these loans, and we never lost a nickel on them." "Harry Brock had a good feel for people who are winners; he knew how to recognize able people without capital," observes Doug Mims, a Central lending officer in the 1960s who later became Alabama's superintendent of banks and then president of his own bank.

Central was also the first bank to recognize the value of Alabama coal when the energy crisis approached in the early 1970s. As prominent Birmingham businessman and civic leader Hall Thompson observes, "Central helped coal miners when they were just coming out of the woodwork. The bank built a great base among the scrappy young coal miners, and they stuck with the bank when the oil embargo hit and coal really went through the roof. Central had coal financing pretty well tied up by the time the other banks got there."

Central's outrageous flair for marketing was more evident in a 1965 campaign to make direct auto loans. Inos Heard, owner of Western Supermarkets, had joined the Central board by this time, and Heard was a Green Stamps believer. He helped Central get the S&H account. Director John Evins came up with the idea of offering Green Stamps with auto loans, and the race was on. Officers at the other banks snickered and sniffed something about "Mickey Mouse," but housewives who normally bought cars with their checkbooks financed some pretty fancy automobiles through Central to get the stamps, Rains reports. The results: 85 car loans, no defaults and only one loan that went past due. "Incentives work," Rains insists.

But by far the most important element in Central's efforts to get good credit customers was a pricing strategy. Prime was sacrosanct in Birmingham, a solid concrete floor under loan rates. The other banks, in their pricing, considered credit quality and the size of the loan but gave no credit for balances kept on deposit. Central saw room for a pricing scheme that would, by giving credit for balances, allow the bank to cut rates, even to below prime, for customers who were essentially borrowing their own money — often the very best customers, the cream of the crop.

So Central introduced "Formula Pricing." From a starting point at prime plus 2 percent, Central would knock off one percentage point from the loan rate for each 20 percent of the loan that was covered by deposit balances; the bank would go as far down as two points below prime. "That was the key," Brock recalls. "It enabled us to pick off one blue-ribbon account after another from the other banks and still have a decent spread."

The other banks faced a real dilemma. They had substantial loan portfolios. To cut their rates meant giving up thousands of dollars of interest income. Not to cut rates meant watching Central take away some of their best customers, one by one. They squirmed and waited and hoped that the account losses would stop, but they didn't. Central was stealing the loan market.

Hjalma Johnson, a former IBM salesman who was hired to take over Brock's old job at Exchange Security and later became president of the Bank of Pasco County, Dade City, Fla., and of the Florida Bankers Association, offers this recollection of what it was like to be on the other side of the fence at this time:

> Central Bank, with no business on its books, had nothing to lose, so it developed a pricing formula, pegged to demand deposits, that allowed below-prime pricing. It would have killed our earnings at Exchange Security to reprice all of our loans, so we didn't. But it finally reached a point where I had to advise the board that we could either bleed to death slowly or bite the bullet and meet the pricing competition. They decided that we couldn't afford to lose any more business, so we repriced. That stopped the outflow, and we were able to hold on to our accounts.
>
> At first we thought Central Bank was a flash, but it kept coming. We said Central had flashy marketing, good connections in Birmingham and good political connections in Montgomery, but no depth of banking skill. We thought they'd move a little business at first and then things would return to normal. But normalcy never returned.
>
> It's easy to rationalize a new competitor's early successes. Old banks always say that new banks are making it on the old banks' turn-downs. This was said about Central, and at first it was believed. Then it was whistling in the dark. Finally we had to admit they were taking our best customers and do something

> to stop them. We began to talk about it at every board meeting and every marketing committee meeting, and we came to agree that after a couple of years of bleeding, this was no scratch, no surface wound that could be patched up in the emergency room overnight. We were in intensive care.

The most conspicuous result of Central's strategy and hustle was radical growth. Central closed out 1964 not with the $8 million in deposits it had projected but with $14 million. It finished 1965 not with $9 million but with $30 million. At the end of 1966 it was not an $11-million bank, as projected, but a $67.7-million one. The bank was growing like wildfire — beyond anyone's expectations.

Central Bank was hard pressed to keep staff growth up with deposit growth, and once again it found a solution to its problem in a way that clashed with the old order: it hired away promising young officers from other Birmingham banks. There was an unwritten rule in Birmingham that no bank would hire another bank's employees. It was a gentleman's rule; it kept competition civilized. It also kept salaries low and bound employees to their banks. Central's rapid growth caught even its own leaders off guard. The need for new employees was often acute. There was neither the time nor the resources for Central to grow its own bankers, so it bought them. Central was able to hire good people because it paid good money and had a reputation as a stimulating place to work. As Jim Lovell, one of the early hire-aways, puts it, "Central could get just about anyone it wanted. If we needed a man, Brock would pay good money to get him, tell him what was wanted, and then turn him loose and let him work. People knew we were having fun, and a lot of them were frustrated at not being able to compete in their old banks because their senior officers wouldn't let them."

It annoyed other banks to recruit and train new officers and then have Central hire them away just as they reached their useful stage, but there was nothing they could do about it. Another Birmingham banking tradition bit the dust.

By the time the bank reached its first birthday, assets had hit $16 million. It was time for some physical expansion. Brock told directors at the April 1965 board meeting that he had secured property at the corner of 20th Street and 7th Avenue South — in the heart of Birmingham's university district, near the University of Alabama at Birmingham — for Central's first branch. By September plans had grown and Central was negotiating with an architect for an office building on the Southside site. By November, the bank had plans for a 14-story, $3.5-million office high-rise. Daniel, who would construct the building, offered the bank a no-lose proposition: if the building filled and was a commercial success, the bank could buy it at cost. If the building did not fill, Daniel Realty would own it and rent space to the bank. The building was completed and opened for business on October 29, 1967, providing breathing room for a bank which had grown to 90 employees by year-end 1966 and had seriously outgrown its downtown office, which became Central's fourth branch.

In August 1966, Central had opened its second and third branch offices. Brock captured good press coverage and managed to create a sense of dynamic expansion by opening them both on the same day and using a helicopter to carry guests and dignitaries from one site to the other during opening ceremonies. It was the first time, the newspapers suggested, that such a thing had been done in Alabama.

Such radical growth created capital strains; the bank was hard pressed to expand its capital as rapidly as its assets and toe the line set by the regulators. By the end of 1964, capital had dropped to 6.7 percent of assets. Growth forced Central to market two stock issues in the same year in 1965. Fortunately, investors adored Central, even though its stock still paid no dividends. Early 1964's $2-a-share stock was selling for about $4.50 by year-end, making Bill Daniel's $10,000 gamble worth $22,500 after only ten months. When Central offered 100,000 new shares for sale in April 1965 for $5 a share, all but 5,244 shares were snatched up by the original investors, who had first rights to the new shares. By November 1965, another 100,000 shares were offered, this time for $10 a share. Original investors grabbed all but 4,657 of them, and Central closed out 1965 with capital at 8.1 percent of assets. Daniel's $10,000 was now worth $50,000, and Brock's $100,000 stock option incentive had grown to $500,000.

Aided by unusually low loan losses and rapid deposit growth, Central moved quickly and permanently into the black. Heavy front end expenses put Central in the red for its first month (March) by $21,902, but the bank moved into the black in April and stayed there. In its history, Central would report only one other month when the bank failed to earn a profit, according to Brock. By June 1964, for example, Central showed a net profit of $12,903.

Monthly Profit and Loss
March 1964

Income		Expenses	
Check Charges	188.21	Advertising	7,883.70
Insurance Premium Income	253.83	Depreciation	1,337.30
Interest on Federal Funds	2,037.02	Insurance	1,191.03
Interest on Installment Loans	1,608.87	Miscellaneous	1,199.33
Interest on Commercial Loans	2,525.70	Interest Paid	1,231.57
Interest on U.S. Securities	11,486.61	Miscellaneous Taxes	3,838.00
Other	513.65	Salaries	16,099.52
		Stationery & Supplies	5,689.73
		Other	2,046.15
Total Income	$18,613.89	Total Expenses	$40,516.33

Net Loss: $21,902.44

June 1964

Income		Expenses	
Check Charges	1,124.10	Advertising	1,796.61
Insurance Premium Income	425.69	Depreciation	1,127.70
Interest on Federal Funds	3,299.49	Insurance	449.58
Interest on Installment Loans	4,667.34	Miscellaneous	408.85
Interest on Commercial Loans	10,519.12	Interest Paid	3,189.73
Interest on U.S. Securities	12,148.02	Miscellaneous Taxes	176.29
Other	906.58	Salaries	8,239.70
		Stationery & Supplies	1,979.07
		Other	2,819.72
Total Income	$33,090.34	Total Expenses	$20,187.25

Net Profit: $12,903.09

1964 Growth

	Deposits	Loans
March 2	$3.7 million	$22,486
April 15	$5.9 million	$1.7 million
June 30	$8.7 million	$3.2 million
September 30	$11.8 million	$4.7 million
December 31	$13.9 million	$6.1 million

Central closed out 1964 solidly in the black, reporting income of $362,412 and expenses of $250,621, for an operating surplus of $111,791, most of which was put into the loan loss reserve. Major income came from loan yields ($181,172) and investment yields ($142,188). Personnel expenses dominated the outflow side of the ledger at $106,312. Interest paid, at $32,358, was modest but still the second largest expense. Advertising for the first year came to $21,809.

The bank's quick profitability was important to its rapid growth. The board agreed that the bank would pay no dividends during its early years so that all of its earnings could be plowed back into its capital account. The more profit Central could pour into capital, the less it would have to sell in the marketplace.

Growth of Contributions to Capital and Reserves from Retained Earnings

1964	1965	1966	1967	1968
$104,600	$307,000	$608,000	$622,000	$866,000
	+195%	+98%	+2%	+39%

The reasons for Central's profit-making in the first few years were different than they would be later. Central made money initially because it was able to corral large amounts of free deposits, operate with very low overhead and avoid loan losses. At the end of 1964, after ten months of operation, $12 million of its $14 million deposits were in checking accounts, which paid no interest, and only $257,000 were in certificates of deposit. Central started with cheap money.

Central had 1965 interest expenses ($118,000) that were only 11.5 percent of its gross operating revenue, while its peers paid 27.5 percent, according to FDIC data. Central spent 19.2 percent of 1965 revenue on salaries, wages and fees, compared to 25.4 percent for its peer group. This large saving in interest expense and modest saving in personnel expense permitted Central to bring 42.6 percent of its revenue to the bottom line (pre-tax), while comparable banks had only 24.7 percent left after expenses.

Despite substantial retained earnings and the two stock offerings in 1965, rapid growth continued to bleed capital ratios. Even after a $543,000 infusion from earnings in 1966, capital stood at 6.2 percent of assets by the end of the year. New capital was essential in 1967. This time Central issued $1.5 million of capital notes, which were again snapped up by the original investors. The notes, which were convertible into common stock, paid 6 percent interest, providing some income to the investors, who had experienced wonderful appreciation but not seen a penny of income so far. The debt issue raised capital to 8 percent of assets by year-end 1967.

Central was scrambling through the early start-up stages, still an inconsequential speck on the Alabama banking picture, when Brock heard some news from Gadsden that would radically alter his game plan. The First National Bank of Gadsden had been sold to State National Bank in Decatur. There was nothing for him to do immediately about these events more than 65 miles away. His plate was full. Nevertheless, he was excited by the news. He could now see the glimmer of a solution to a future problem. That merger would have great consequences for Central Bank.

By June 29, 1968, Central closed the books on 52 months of business with assets of $81,690,515, deposits of $72,974,256, and a 7-percent share of the Birmingham market. It had elbowed its way into a still minor but statistically significant position in the Birmingham market. More significantly, it had changed the way banking was done and had stimulated other banks into being more competitive to protect their markets. Central, in its enthusiasm, probably held exaggerated notions of how it was single-handedly reforming the industry, but Central had introduced changes which stuck. Birmingham had been puzzled, provoked and even shocked by the upstart. Central and its CEO had earned a maverick label and were controversial within Jefferson County but were known elsewhere in the state only as a convivial correspondent bank.

People said that Central was audacious, that Brock was highly ambitious. But what happened in July 1968 sent shock waves throughout the state. It was more audacious and ambitious than almost anyone expected. It shook banking in Alabama to the core and set in motion a series of far-reaching reactions. In Alabama, as had happened in Birmingham, normalcy would never return.

CHAPTER FOUR

The Bait Swallows The Fish

ON SATURDAY MORNING, July 13, 1968, Schuyler Baker was ready to leave Birmingham for a day at the lake when Harry Brock got hold of him. He spent the rest of the day and much of the night on the telephone, calling everyone he had ever met or heard of who owned shares of stock in State National Bank, the third largest bank in Alabama. He was trying to buy their shares.

◇

On Sunday, July 14, Frederick Deane, the president of the Bank of Virginia, returned from church to his Richmond home and took a call from Harry Brock. Brock wanted to borrow $10 million to finance the unfriendly takeover of a bank in north Alabama. Deane understood what was happening and agreed to advance the money.

◇

Shortly after midnight on Monday, July 15, Joyce Agricola Parker was awakened in Gadsden by a telephone call and was asked to come next door, to her father's house. There she found her father, Hugh Agricola; her husband, Hugh Parker, and Harry Brock. They wanted her to sign a long legal document called a voting trust. "You can read it first if you want to," her husband joked. She signed the papers and went back to bed.

◇

On Monday morning, July 15, Willard Nelson came to work at his bank in Decatur as usual. Nelson was president of

State National Bank. With branches in 12 north Alabama counties, State National was blessed with one of the richest franchises in the state and had recently grown to be the third largest. Nelson was also president of the Alabama Bankers Association. Later that morning he was visited by Harry Brock, who told him that he had seized working control of the stock of State National. Nelson found that hard to believe, but his trust officer soon confirmed that Brock did indeed have the Buttrey stock and that the Agricolas were with him. It was the kind of shock that few men entirely get over, and Nelson was no exception.

◇

These episodes were part of a rapid-fire series of events that started when Agricola called Brock on Thursday, July 11, to tell him, in effect, that it was now or never. Suddenly the time was once again right for something Brock had thought about doing for a long time. The State National board had opened negotiations with a group of Birmingham bankers and investors about forming a multibank holding company. Unless Brock intervened, they were likely to close a deal at the board meeting the next Tuesday, Agricola said.

That phone call set off five frantic days in July that saw Brock and the Central crowd scrambling like they had never scrambled before. By the end of those days, they had done the unthinkable. They had executed an unfriendly takeover of a bank, something that had never happened in Alabama, at least not in recent history. And they had taken over a bank that was nearly two and a half times larger than Central. Beyond even that, they had grabbed the richest prize in the whole state, the bank everyone wanted. It was, for Brock, his moment of greatest triumph. In the eyes of other bankers around the state, it was an act of piracy.

State National was a proud old bank with a long tradition. Its offices stretched across north Alabama, which, in the 1960s, was the fastest growing part of the state. And State National had something which no other Alabama bank had or was allowed by law to have: branches outside its home county. State National in 1968 had branches in 12 counties. Moreover, it had a history of moving its branches around — closing a branch in a tiny backwater area in order to reincarnate it in a more attractive market, often in a different county. There was a mystique about State National. It had a "unique charter," people said. They rarely talked about it without some allusion to its past and its special branching rights.

What it had was an old charter, one dating back to 1892, when it was incorporated as The Merchants Bank in Florence. It had moved to Decatur in 1906. Prior to 1911, Alabama banks were allowed to branch at will. Most banks chose not to branch, but one of the exceptions was Merchants, which in 1908 changed its name to Tennessee Valley Bank. There a banking pioneer named S. S. Broadus opened a string of small bank offices in a series of north Alabama villages more or less along the Tennessee River. By 1911, there were 15 branches in eight counties.

In 1911, branch banking became an issue, and the Alabama legislature outlawed branching but left the door open for a county or city that wanted branching to seek local-option legislation to permit branching within its boundaries.

> From and after the passage of this act, no bank, or any officer, agent, or director thereof, shall be permitted to establish a branch or office for the transaction of the banking business, other than at its principal place of business.

So the law read. State National's charter said nothing at all about branching. By its date, however, it gave Merchants/ Tennessee Valley the same powers as all state chartered banks at that time, which included branching. The State National branching rights were validated less by its charter than by the phrase "from and after the passage of this act" in the 1911 bill, which did not make the law retroactive but "grandfathered" the branches of the then Tennessee Valley Bank.

Of the handful of Alabama banks that had grandfathered branching systems, all were closed during the Depression. Tennessee Valley Bank, like many banks at that time, became insolvent and went into receivership. But through the efforts of some Decatur businessmen, the bank was reorganized in 1934 under the same 1892 charter and with the same branches it had before it was closed. This arrangement was subsequently approved by the Alabama Supreme Court in 1936. When it converted to a national bank in 1939, Tennessee Valley Bank received from the U.S. Comptroller of the Currency certificates showing authority to operate branches in 13 cities besides Decatur.

Both before and after its reorganization, the bank entered new towns in new counties, often through merger with an existing bank, but after 1911, whenever it branched across county lines, it closed one office for each new entry to support the pretext that it was not adding branches, only moving them. The legal basis for such moves was unclear. State National's attorneys, Norman and Julian Harris, recall going to Montgomery (probably in 1940) to seek an opinion from the state attorney general on the legality of relocating branches. Attorney General Thomas S. Lawson was of the opinion that branches could legally be moved, but his top assistant thought they could not. So Lawson issued a favorable opinion, and the bank simply assumed the power and went ahead and moved branches around as it wanted to, always subject to approval by the state banking department and, after it became a national bank in 1939, by the Comptroller of the Currency. It was never challenged.

These exotic branching rights caught Brock's eye while he was still an officer of Exchange Security. If State National could merge with a bank in Huntsville or Oneonta or Fort Payne, why couldn't it do so in Montgomery, Mobile and Tuscaloosa? If a Birmingham bank could get State National, it could build a statewide system, and the only one that would be legal in Alabama, Brock reasoned. He asked Jim Simpson, the Exchange Security director, for permission to spend a Saturday afternoon in his law library to do a little research. Finally Brock convinced Simpson that they should give the merger a try, so the two of them went up to Decatur to talk about a possible merger. State National's officials politely let them know that they were not interested in merging with a Birmingham bank, and the matter was dropped — by all but Brock, anyway. He kept mulling over the problem: how do you marry someone who won't have you?

Brock thought he saw a way in 1964 when State National

acquired the First National Bank of Gadsden. Brock had grown up in Gadsden, and was well acquainted with Hugh Agricola, Sr., who owned much of the stock of First National of Gadsden. The merger made Agricola vice chairman of State National's board. Agricola was a shrewd trader and had bargained for a healthy premium: while First National of Gadsden contributed only 16 percent of the earnings of the post-merger bank, its shareholders got 20 percent of the stock. Brock was elated to find that one-fifth of the stock of State National was now in hands that were potentially friendly to him, more than half of which was controlled by Agricola and members of his family.

Though Brock was up to his ears in things to do to get his own new bank up and running, he began to lay the groundwork for consummating a merger with State National — one way or another. He made it a point to cultivate three people whose help he was likely to need. One was Agricola. Another was Wilson Taylor, a director who owned a substantial amount of State National stock. The third was Roscoe Buttrey, a Nashville banker (later president of Third National Bank) who was an officer of the Crescent Amusement Co., a movie theater chain owned by the Sudicam family. Buttrey was also investment manager for the Mutual Savings Life Insurance Co., which was located in Decatur. Both Crescent and Mutual Savings had sizeable amounts of State National stock in their portfolios. Brock stayed in touch with these three people and made sure they were familiar with what Central Bank was doing. And he touched on his interest in getting control of State National, at least with Buttrey and Agricola.

The merger with the Gadsden bank brought Agricola and his son-in-law, Hugh Parker, into the management of State National. Parker, a West Point graduate, left the military when he saw that he had arrived too late for World War II and would always labor in the shadows of its combat veterans. He set out to make a career in banking after his marriage. He was interested in capitalizing on the special privileges State National enjoyed. Willard Nelson, State National's president, was regarded by his colleagues as moderately progressive. He had come up through the ranks and been brought back from the Sheffield branch to be groomed for the presidency. He had started a trust department, an audit department, a fledgling marketing department and a loan examination department. He had automated operations. He had brought in a couple of young bankers from Memphis, Billy Hunter and Bill Collins. "Willard Nelson took over a bunch of country banks and slowly but surely was building them into a sophisticated organization," Hunter reflects.

Gadsden had been State National's first territorial expansion since 1946, but Nelson and Parker did not intend for it to be their last. Parker reportedly made at least one trip to New York to consult with investment bankers about acquisitions. Nelson recalls some form of merger discussion with First of Montgomery, First of Anniston, Alabama National of Montgomery, Henderson National of Huntsville and the J. C. Jacobs Banking Co. of Scottsboro. By 1968, a lot of preliminary discussions were going on. Brock's old colleagues from Exchange Security still wanted to "get together" with State National and had set up an exploratory meeting at a safe spot during the spring of 1968. Parker, Nelson, Taylor and J. W. "Billy" Wyker, Jr., chairman of the State National board, met with Simpson, Pless, and William Sellers from Exchange Security at the Holiday Inn in Cullman, according to Parker's recollection. The Exchange Security delegation tried to sell the Decatur people on a merger between the two banks. A follow-up meeting took place one afternoon in Simpson's law offices in Birmingham, probably in April. Simpson steered the subject toward specifics: where the headquarters would be, who would serve on the board, and who would be general counsel. The State National representatives were a little put off by what they perceived as Birmingham dominance. The meeting ended inconclusively. The State National representatives were not empowered to negotiate for the bank. After the meeting, Parker and Nelson shared their reservations. Both anticipated personality conflicts, Parker later recalled in an affidavit taken in 1969. The matter was left hanging at this point. No decision was ever made by the State National board.

The Exchange Security proposal actually went on a back burner as State National's leaders became more interested in another offer. Even before the meeting in Cullman with Exchange Security officials, Parker and Agricola had been visited in Gadsden by Hugh Morrow, Jr., a Birmingham investment banker; his son Hugh Morrow III, and Lewis Odess, a Birmingham stockbroker. The Morrows and Odess were major stockholders in the City National Bank of Tuscaloosa and had organized a City National Bank in Birmingham about a year after Central had opened. They wanted the Agricola family to help them arrange a merger between State National and one or both of their banks, according to Parker. Agricola did nothing for a while, despite repeated visits by the Morrows, then brought up the subject at a State National board meeting. Other directors objected to entering negotiations with the Morrows, and the matter was dropped.

But it came up again late in the spring of 1968, and this time the contact was made, not through the Agricolas, but through Ronald Williams, a former C&S correspondent banker who was now State National's marketing officer. He was also a personal friend of Hugh Morrow III. Encouraged by Nelson, Williams explored a possible deal with the Morrows. This time the plan was to form Alabama's first multibank holding company with State National and the two City Nationals as members. Decatur would have been the headquarters, State National the lead bank, Nelson says.

Multibank holding companies had been on the scene since about 1900 and had grown dramatically after World War II, leading to federal legislation in 1956 defining (and limiting) their powers. There were none in Alabama, but they were beginning to appear in Virginia and Florida. The number of bank holding companies increased from 53 to 121 between 1965 and 1970 and increased their share of U.S. deposits from 8.3 to 16.2 percent. Since Alabama's banking laws did not prohibit bank holding companies, they could legally be formed. It was only a matter of time before some Alabama bank or group of banks began to put together a large organization using the multibank holding company vehicle.

The Morrows almost took this historic step. Their holding company proposal was arousing serious interest in Decatur. The State National board, on July 9, 1968, authorized negotiations with the Morrows and hired an accountant to look into stock valuation.

Weeks earlier, rumors that a deal was shaping up in

Decatur had reached the First National Bank of Birmingham, and Parker received one of those "talk to us before you do anything" calls from Harvey "Red" Terrell, First's vice-chairman. Parker stopped at First National to see Terrell, who asked him to talk to John Hand. Hand indicated that he would like to affiliate State National with First, either by merger or through a holding company, but feared that such a deal would spark anti-trust action because First was still by far the largest bank in the state.

It is not clear just how close State National and the Morrows were to an agreement. George LeMaistre, president of Morrow's City National Bank in Tuscaloosa, recalls that Hugh Morrow, Jr., came away thinking a deal had been made and lined up his financing with John Hand. Both Nelson and Taylor indicate that a deal was imminent, although negotiations had been handled mostly through Williams, and the Morrows had their first face-to-face meeting with Nelson, Taylor and Wyker just prior to the July 9 board meeting. Agricola certainly told Brock that he hadn't much time to block the Morrow deal. Yet Williams insists that negotiations never got past the tentative, exploratory stage, that matters like headquarters location, officer and board slots and stock exchange ratios had not even been discussed. And Wyker, who was certainly a strong voice in State National's leadership, had objections to the Morrows and thinks that there would have been no deal with them.

At any rate, Brock thought that the chance of a lifetime was about to slip from his grasp, so he rocketed into action. He had suspected for years that State National management would resist merger with a stronger bank and that the only way to get it would be by controlling enough stock to force a merger. Now he knew that the only certain way he could block a deal with the Morrows was to grab enough stock so that management would be unable to make any deals without his consent. He was going after the stock.

State National had 350,000 shares outstanding. It was widely distributed, with few large blocks to be found. That was a mixed blessing for Brock. It made it hard to buy up a lot of stock quickly, but it also made it hard for anyone else to line up enough stock to stop him. If he could get 40 percent of the stock, he decided, he would have working control of the bank. That became his goal. The Agricolas would be essential. The old First National Bank of Gadsden shareholders held nearly 20 percent of the State National stock. The Agricola family itself controlled 35,000 shares or 10 percent of the total, and Hugh Agricola was the key to getting more of the other 10 percent linked to the Gadsden bank.

He also had to have Buttrey. Crescent Amusement held 20,200 shares and Mutual Savings Life 11,200. If he could persuade Buttrey to sell him both blocks of stock, he would have another 31,400 shares, another 9 percent. That would give him somewhere between 25 and 30 percent — an imposing start and probably enough to block the Morrow deal but still short of working control. The last 10 to 15 percent would have to be accumulated slowly in bits and pieces, but he needed it.

The takeover would be expensive. State National stock was selling for $51 at the time. If he had to pay $75 a share to get 40 percent of the stock, the cost would be more than $10 million. He had to assemble an investor group, find people to buy the stock as well as people to sell it. He did not call a meeting of the Central board. It would be better in this case, he decided, not to officially involve the bank but to work through a private investor group. So he called Daniel, Baker, Israel, Welch, Hardy, Heard, and Wendell Taylor, as well as Tom Jernigan, Wally Nall, Marshall Durbin, and John Evins, who by this time were members of the Central board. He explained the situation to them. They were all ready to back him, although they differed in their enthusiasm for the project and their available cash. Jernigan, who had recently sold a company, was flush; he and Durbin were prepared to be major investors. Daniel had misgivings about the unfriendly takeover and anticipated a strong negative reaction. He also had to be convinced that it would be a good buy even if it couldn't be used, as Brock was excitedly explaining, to be a springboard for Alabama's first and only statewide branching system. He would help finance the takeover, Daniel decided, but not as a major investor.

The Central group was once again the nucleus, but this project would require additional help, Brock knew. Atlanta's conglomerateur J. B. Fuqua was approached but decided not to join. Brock had better luck with Jimmy Hays and Ed Lowder. Hays was president of the Alabama Farm Bureau; Lowder was its treasurer and head of its insurance company. Hays was also a substantial Huntsville area farmer, and Lowder was already gaining a reputation as a financial wizard and bank stock investor. They were ready and willing to take a full piece of the action. In fact Lowder and Hays were willing to take half of the stock Brock could get, Lowder recalls, and Brock had to encourage other investors so that Lowder and Hays wouldn't have too dominant a stake.

Brock had already looked into the financing for his takeover. He remembered well his rejection in Atlanta when he needed to borrow $1 million to launch Central. Next time, he told himself, he would find a bank well outside his deep-South region, one that would not worry about heat from his uptown rivals. He found his banker in Rick Deane. It was at a Young Presidents Organization gathering in Freeport, in the Bahamas, in January 1968, that Brock first approached Deane. He was already thinking about a takeover attempt on State National and outlined his plan to Deane, who was himself experiencing the beginnings of statewide holding companies in Virginia. Deane thought Brock was in step with the times.

On Sunday, July 14, as Brock was frantically assembling the pieces for his assault, he called Deane at his home and reminded him of their conversation in the Bahamas. Brock quickly gave Deane the pertinent details, and Deane gave Brock a verbal commitment over the phone. The next day Deane went to work in his bank and mentioned to his superior, Chairman Herbert Moseley, "Herb, I committed us to a $10-million loan yesterday."

Moseley, Deane recalls, said, "Maybe you'd better tell me about it." Deane convinced his boss that the loan was solid. "You could tell from what Harry had done at Central that he would be successful with his plan," Deane explains. Brock, on his part, recalls that he was cautious enough or intuitive enough to ask for a two-year commitment.

The loan was an available line of credit which Brock's group could tap at will to pay for State National stock they could acquire. The loans would be held by various members of the investment group, secured by the stock they were buying.

All the State National stock that was acquired, at prices ranging from $70 to $85.50 a share, was pooled and then divided among the investors at the average price of $78.85 a share. A full participation in the investment pool was 7,525 shares of State National stock. Brock took a full share. So did Durbin and Jernigan from the Central board and Hays and Lowder from outside the board. Daniel, Baker, Israel, Evins and Dr. Taylor each took a half-participation, Hardy and Heard a quarter share each, and Welch an eighth.

Primed to buy stock, Brock telephoned Buttrey. He offered him $70 a share for the stock he controlled. It was trading that day for $51. But Brock found Buttrey, who knew what Brock was up to, hard to deal with. The best Brock could get was a six-day option on the Crescent stock for $5 a share and outright sale of the Mutual Savings shares. He sent a courier to Nashville with his check to tie down the Buttrey stock. So far so good.

As president of the Crescent Amusement Co., Buttrey had authority to sell the stock, and $70 per share plus $5 for the option looked like a good price, so he sold. As investment manager for Mutual Savings Life, he needed to consult with its president, Redus Collier. Collier, in turn, ran the deal by one of his directors, Billy Wyker, since Wyker was also chairman of the board of State National. An original director of the reorganized bank as it emerged from the 1930s, Wyker was a member of the inner circle at State National. He was a proud citizen of Decatur and a staunchly upright man who liked his business deals to be straightforward and aboveboard. He would not knowingly have helped a Birmingham upstart take over his bank.

But Wyker had been felled by a heart attack in April while attending the Masters Golf Tournament in Augusta. He spent three weeks in an Augusta hospital, then came home for six more weeks of rest. He was away from business, from meetings, from street-corner conversations, from coffee breaks. He had just returned to board meetings at the time negotiations with the Morrows were authorized, and he had picked up no rumors about takeover attempts. Wyker never heard why someone wanted the stock for $70, so, instead of asking Mutual Savings Life to hold onto the stock, Wyker agreed that $70 was a fine price and approved the sale as a sensible investment decision for Mutual Savings Life.

Baker, Rains and a few others worked the phones over the weekend, trying to buy additional State National shares from anyone they knew who owned any, but they had little success and raised more curiosity than stock for their efforts.

Brock still needed to get the Agricola stock in the bag. He had been coaxing Hugh Agricola for several years, using all his persuasive powers to convince Agricola of the rosier future State National would enjoy if it could be put together with Central and infused with the Central spirit of aggressive competition and expansion. He knew very well that Agricola had no intention of selling his stock. He needed to convince Agricola to sign a voting trust, to retain the beneficial ownership of the stock but assign the voting control to a trust, where all the Agricola stock and stock the Brock group could acquire would be voted in a block by the trustees.

The voting trust contained provisions for trustees and voting rights, but it also became a contract between the Brock group and the Agricolas. The Agricolas placed the 35,000 shares they controlled in the trust and agreed to deliver another 15,000. Brock pledged to deliver the Buttrey stock and to make a tender offer at $70 per share until he had accumulated enough to bring the total to 40 percent. Agricola was still concerned that the plan might not work, so Brock had to include a promise to buy out the Agricolas at $85 a share if he was unable to come up with his part of the stock within two years.

By the time all the negotiating was done and the papers drawn up, it was late Sunday evening. There was some concern that the legality of the trust might be challenged if it was signed on Sunday, so everyone sat around in Agricola's house until after midnight and then signed, calling Joyce Parker over from next door so she could sign the document.

It was late when Brock returned home from Gadsden, only hours before he would leave for Decatur, but he didn't go straight to bed. Jane remembers him sitting at her dressing table in the middle of the night, trying to figure out how he could most gently break the news to Willard Nelson.

Brock picked up Jernigan early Monday morning, July 15, and the two of them flew to Decatur in Jernigan's plane. Their first stop would be for Wilson Taylor. Taylor was the largest Decatur shareholder on the State National board, with some 12,000 shares. He was also the friendliest to Brock, aside from the Agricolas. Taylor understood Brock's interest, liked Brock personally, admired the success that Central had carved out in Birmingham, and he could be counted on to take a calm view of the takeover — possibly even an optimistic one. Brock considered Taylor a tacit supporter.

Taylor was not at home when Brock called, but Mrs. Taylor came to meet them at the airport and drove them to a motel one block down the street from the bank. Taylor, who had been contacted by his wife, met them there, and Brock asked if they could get a private room. There he opened the conversation by offering to buy Taylor's stock for $80 a share. Taylor refused and also declined to promise to vote with Brock. "These are my friends here. I can't do that," Taylor recalls explaining to Brock. Brock asked Taylor to go to the bank, break the news to Nelson, and ask for a meeting. Taylor agreed to this. Nelson was skeptical, doubting that a takeover could have been executed, but agreed to meet with Brock, so Taylor called Brock and told him to come on over.

They gathered in the bank's penthouse for a confrontation Taylor describes as "very exciting, very sobering to top management. They were quite surprised." Brock claimed to have 25 percent of the stock, which was a bit of a bluff. He actually had closer to 20, but the State National leaders readily believed that the Agricolas could deliver 50,000 shares, so they accepted Brock's account. Brock asked for a shareholder list. Nelson was advised by the Harrises, the bank's attorneys, that as a major stockholder Brock was entitled to the list. It was not a long meeting or an acrimonious one. The arguing would come later.

Brock, Jernigan and Taylor left the bank and called on Wyker at his house, where he was still recuperating from his heart attack. Then they called on a few local shareholders and were able to buy a little more stock before Brock and Jernigan returned to Birmingham.

The events of the day left State National in shock. No one among the directors or senior officers welcomed the takeover. There was talk of fighting it, but the opposition simply did not crystallize. "I had mixed emotions," Taylor recalls. "I would rather have Harry Brock as a partner than Hugh Morrow, but my loyalty to State National was paramount. I loved State National. I was not all for Brock's group, but I was excited by his plan and the idea that he might be right about this being the thing to do. With the right leadership and more of an effort to head off the takeover, it could have been blocked." Yet it was Taylor who called John Hand at First of Birmingham to enlist Hand's aid in beating the takeover. Hand suggested that such efforts would be "fruitless," that it was too late, Taylor recalls, but Hand added, "I sure wish I could help you out."

Wyker was strongly opposed to the takeover, but he was in no shape to lead a protracted battle. Brock would be a tough adversary, and he had a big head start. "If our north Alabama group had really wanted to bow our necks and stop the merger, we could have gone on the market and tried to buy enough stock to keep control," he says, "but no one here was willing to fight it on a purchase basis." While Wyker hated to lose the bank, he admitted a kind of reluctant admiration for what the Birmingham group had done. "If you had guts enough to buy enough stock for control and we didn't, you can go ahead," he remembers saying to Brock. "I could find no fault with the Birmingham group," he now says. "It was an entirely honest deal."

Nelson is described by colleagues as seeming dazed by the news. He was 59 at the time and concerned about what would happen to him personally. When the State National board acted on July 18, it was to renegotiate its contract with Nelson, offering him a five-year contract and raising his salary to $50,000 annually. The contract would be binding even after a merger, the Harrises assured the board. They had given up the cause and were trying to salvage individuals.

At that same Thursday board meeting, with Wyker

absent, the directors voted to send the following letter, over Nelson's signature, to shareholders:

> The Board of Directors of State National Bank of Alabama wishes to advise you that a group of individuals in Birmingham is making a concerted effort to acquire a substantial interest of stock in State National Bank. This activity has caused a considerable increase in the market price of the stock.
>
> The Board can not quote you a price on your stock but it is the opinion of the individual members of the Board that the stock has for many months been selling below its reasonable value. It appears that $70.00 per share is a fair price for the stock at this time.
>
> Naturally the Board would prefer that the Bank continue as it is presently constituted. It has confidence in the continued growth and progress of the Bank thus increasing the value of your stock. Certainly North Alabama is the most prosperous and fastest growing area in the State. It is our feeling that each shareholder should evaluate his own position.

Brock knew exactly what he had to do. The bomb had gone off on schedule. There was confusion in the enemy camp. He had taken the hill, but now he had to secure it. He had to get at least another 15 percent of the State National stock. He called in Goodbody & Co., a stock brokerage concern that was one of his tenants in the new Central Bank building, and ordered a 36-hour public tender offer at $70 per share. He also called together some Central employees, Lovell recalls, gave them shareholder lists and sent them off to the telephones. The bushes were being beaten.

The story hit the newspapers on Thursday, July 18. All Alabama was abuzz about the coup. Shareholders, sensing a battle, held on to their stock, and the first tender offer attracted only about 7,000 shares. Everyone, Brock included, was waiting to see what the Morrows would do. On July 19, they weighed in with a tender offer at $80 per share, limited to 30 days and contingent on their receiving at least 150,000 shares of the stock. That tender offer could hardly have achieved its objectives, even if Brock had let it go unchallenged. He didn't. Having smoked out the competition, Brock countered with his big tender offer, the one that would ultimately put him over the top.

Brock was reluctant to use the largest brokerage house in

Birmingham, Sterne, Agee & Leach, because he knew it had close ties to First National. But Jernigan, who was himself a Sterne, Agee customer, convinced Brock to give it a try. The firm had handled stock issues for State National in the past and knew better than anyone else how to find those most likely to sell. So Brock got together with Mervyn Sterne. His group would buy any available State National stock at a price over $80 but not more than $85, Brock explained. They agreed on a 50-cents-per-share commission for Sterne, Agee, and Sterne put his troops to work. Brock put no time limit on his offer.

At this price, significant amounts of stock began to move, particularly when it became evident that the Morrows were bowing out. "We could have had it if we had wanted it badly enough," Dr. John Odess, a member of the Morrow group, recalls, "but Harry Brock came along and borrowed a lot of money and was willing to pay more for it than we were."

Lowder recalls being the contact man for the investor group during this period. Sterne would repeatedly call him as they acquired stock, report the amount and the price, and ask for authorization to make further buys. The Central group was getting close to the 40 percent they were seeking. One of the largest blocks still outstanding was controlled by the trust department of First National Bank of Birmingham. Brock regarded Hand as a certain opponent. However, the State National stock was not in the bank's investment portfolio but in the portfolios of its trust customers, including its own employee pension fund. The bank had a fiduciary responsibility to act in the best interest of its customers, and $85 a share was a high price for State National stock. Brock was concerned that First National would try to hold onto the shares, but Harold F. Miller, Jr., who managed First National's trust investments at that time, reports that there was no pressure from management. At any rate, First National sold its stock. "You've got it now," Sterne told Lowder, and Brock noted the irony of the biggest bank in the state providing the crucial stock that he believed would make Central the biggest bank in the state.

The battle for control of State National stock was over, four long weeks after it began. Brock had won. He planned to move quickly to merge Central and State National, then capitalize on the branching powers he had paid so dearly to acquire to open offices in Mobile, Montgomery, Tuscaloosa and the other most financially attractive centers in the state. Central would be the first statewide bank in Alabama and enjoy the pioneer's rights to claim the best of the new territory. And even before the statewide system was built, Central, after the merger, would be a $300-million bank, the third largest in the state and only $42 million behind second-place BTNB. Four and a half years ago he had been stuffing checking account statements into envelopes while most of Birmingham waited for the new bank to go under. Now Brock contemplated himself as chief of one of Alabama's Big Three. He liked it.

But first he had to effect a merger. State National was a captive nation. Brock had taken the citadel with a dazzling show of force, but he had yet to win the hearts and minds of the people. Preliminary discussions with Hunter and Collins had gone well. They would work with him, Brock correctly surmised. And Parker and Agricola were already his partners. But Nelson and the rest of the State National board were proud men who had been unexpectedly humbled. The yoke of captivity sat heavily on them. They were resentful, potentially rebellious. Brock would have to win them over, convert them to happy, enthusiastic, productive members of his team. In the meantime, he would need to keep them in line without further antagonizing them.

Brock quickly learned that getting the State National board to see things his way would be no picnic when he brought the two bank boards literally together on September 16. The Central directors met at 9 a.m. in Birmingham to approve a few loans, then drove up to Decatur for the real business of the day: a joint meeting with the State National board at 11:30.

Brock endeavored to push through a merger agreement between the two organizations, and made good progress on some of the major points. State National directors agreed to a stock exchange ratio recommended by New York investment banker Harry Keefe, head of Keefe, Bruyette & Woods, who had been brought in to give an objective, professional opinion of the proper ratio for issuing stock in the merged organization.

Keefe had recommended that State National shareholders get five shares of Central stock for each State National share — reflecting the approximate difference in the book value and market prices of the two bank stocks. State National directors were ready to accept this ratio, which would give their shareholders 68.5 percent of the shares of the new bank (actually only 66.6 percent if Central's convertible notes were converted to 75,485 shares of common stock, as in fact they were). They also agreed to operate under Central's charter and keep the headquarters in Birmingham, a position almost forced by Jefferson County's branching laws. Moreover, they agreed that each of the 11 State National directors and 12 Central directors should be included in the 23-member board of the new bank.

But State National's board wanted the surviving bank to be a national bank, and they wanted it called State National Bank. Brock and Nelson debated the advantages of a state or national charter, and the two boards went into separate sessions to hammer out their merger positions. The State National board voted unanimously to approve the merger — with a 5-to-1 exchange ratio, Birmingham headquarters and 23-member board — *if* Central converted to a national bank and the resulting bank were named State National Bank of Alabama. Central directors, meanwhile, followed Brock's wishes and approved a merger plan calling for a state-chartered bank to be known as Central State Bank of Alabama.

The Central directors rejoined the State National directors for another joint session. When Brock heard the State National resolution, according to the Central minutes, he "made a short statement in which he expressed disappointment that there was apparently no consideration given a name which would retain some part of the name of both banks, which has been done many times in a merger in order to please both sides. Furthermore, Mr. Brock expressed concern that the decision to eliminate the possibility of a state chartered bank was not to the best interest of the majority of the stockholders, and therefore he could not ignore a half million dollars per year in extra earnings which the bank would lose if they chose a National Charter." Then everyone went home.

Brock did not intend to concede either of the contested points. The choice of a state or national charter would prove to have serious, unexpected legal ramifications, but in the summer of 1968, it was largely an economic and regulatory issue to Brock. State banks had broader lending powers and higher legal lending limits on secured loans, could pay dividends with fewer regulatory constraints and had lighter reporting requirements. Moreover, state banks were exempt from the non-earning reserves required from Fed members. Loss of earnings on the reserves, Brock calculated with the help of three members of the State National staff, would cost the merged bank $523,250 a year in net earnings after taxes. So he had a talk with Agricola and Parker, and at State National's next board meeting, on October 8, 1968, Parker made a motion to reconsider State National's merger resolution; Agricola seconded the motion. It was soundly defeated, with only Parker and Agricola voting for reconsideration, and the other nine directors voting against it.

It was time for some serious arm twisting and horse trading. By the time the State National board met in special session eight days later, on October 16, some positions had changed. Parker again made his motion for reconsideration, and this time was seconded by Taylor. A vote this time produced seven yeas and three abstentions. Parker then moved that State National approve a merger under Central's charter with the understanding that Nelson would be CEO. His motion said nothing about a state or national charter, but did propose that "the name of the bank be The Bank of Alabama, or if this is not agreeable, State Central Bank of Alabama." This motion also passed by a 7-0 vote with three abstentions.

There were further problems in November — serious enough to break off negotiations. Wyker has letters he exchanged with Daniel that month in an effort by the two chairmen to get discussions moving again. Wyker visited Daniel on a trip to Birmingham to see his heart specialist, and negotiations were resumed.

The merger plan finally hammered out and adopted on December 13 for presentation to shareholders of both banks kept Brock's proposed name of Central State Bank and the state charter, but the name was quickly switched to Central Bank and Trust at a special meeting on December 23. Legal difficulties had arisen because there was already a Central State Bank in Calera, Ala., Brock told his directors. To avoid the possibility of legal challenge, they should keep one of the two names to which they held clear rights, Brock argued. Since it would be illegal to call a state-chartered bank State National, the logical choice was Central Bank and Trust. The State National board was cornered and conceded the point.

Central's only major concession came in the restructured management of the new bank. Nelson would be named chairman and chief executive; Brock would be designated president and chief administrative officer. Daniel would step down to vice chairman of the board, and Wyker would also be a vice chairman and would be chairman of the executive committee. All directors of the two banks would serve on the new board, and the stock would be exchanged at five Central shares for each State National share.

This exchange ratio gave Central shareholders a 24-percent premium over the stock's September 30, 1968, book value, while State National stock would exchange at an 8.4-percent discount to book. Central, which would provide 29 percent of the merged bank's assets, 30.4 percent of its capital and 33.6 percent of its earnings, would receive 31.4 percent of the stock.

The exchange ratio in 1968 was not controversial. It had been accepted by both sides since the September joint meeting. While none of the State National directors owned Central stock, all but one of Central's directors had become major State National shareholders during the takeover. In fact, four of Central's directors — Durbin, Jernigan, Heard and Evins — had more money in State National stock than they had in Central stock. Lowder and Hays were also major State National shareholders as a result of their roles in the takeover. Conventional appraisal methods could not capture such imponderables as State National's unique branching rights and Central's meteoric growth, but the exchange ratio was accepted by most of the principal parties.

Side by side, the two banks presented an interesting combination of similarities and differences.

Two-Bank Financial Comparison

	Central	State National
Total Assets (9/30/68)	$83 million	$202 million
Asset Growth (9/30/67-9/30/68)	28.60%	12.40%
Deposit Growth (9/30/67-9/30/68)	25.80%	11.90%
Loans to Deposits (9/30/68)	52.80%	55.30%
Capital to Assets (9/30/68)	7.86%	7.41%
1967 Return on Assets	0.96%	1.21%
1968 Return on Assets	1.01%	1.38%
1967 Return on Equity	12.11%	17.14%
1968 Return on Equity	13.14%	19.60%

Both were growing rapidly and profitably. State National had 25 offices in 12 counties; Central had six offices in one county. State National served a rural area and had a retail and agricultural orientation. Central served a city and had urban, wholesale, commercial characteristics. Central had a more urban, more entrepreneurial pay scale. Brock made $56,911 in 1967, while Nelson, prior to his new contract, made only $35,774 in 1967, according to the proxy statement issued in anticipation of the merger. Central still had the cheaper deposit base: 73.5 percent demand deposits, 13 percent savings and only 13.5 percent time money, while State National had 56.6 percent demand, 14.3 percent savings and 29 percent time.

The process of arriving at the merger agreement had been difficult, but the differences between the two banks were finally resolved in a largely amicable fashion. While the issues had not been settled to everyone's satisfaction, the boards and managements of both banks were solidly behind the merger plan that was printed, dated December 27, 1968, and mailed to the shareholders. A special shareholders' meeting was called for January 28, 1969, when shareholders of each bank would be asked to approve the merger plan. If two-thirds approved, only the approvals of the state banking superintendent and the FDIC were needed, and the merger was an accomplished fact. It seemed very close, but it would take 12 turbulent years of struggle to bring it about.

CHAPTER FIVE

The Empire Strikes Back

BROCK'S SUCCESSFUL RAID on Decatur had thoroughly alarmed the bankers of Alabama. The sometimes annoying, sometimes engaging upstart had become a public menace. Stealing Nelson's bank away was a shocking affront to the professional courtesy that kept banking a civilized occupation, they felt. A statewide banking system threatened Alabama's long devotion to keeping bank ownership and control in local communities, an emotional issue over which community bankers were prepared to go to war. A statewide system also threatened the major urban banks of the state. It would give to a single competitor too great an advantage. Central was stretching a loophole so that it could operate outside the intended banking laws of Alabama, the laws which bound everyone else. This time Brock had gone too far, most of the state's bankers thought. It was time to nail his hide to the wall, and one of the first to show up with a hammer was Jim Simpson.

Long before Brock moved to take over State National, he had satisfied himself that it could legally be done. The 1911 bill unambiguously banned a bank from operating any office other than its home office, with exceptions granted only under local-option legislation. (Birmingham banks, for example, were permitted to branch within Jefferson County.) State National had been allowed to keep branches predating the 1911 law, but the merger plan called for State National to become a branch of Central, not vice versa. Would the State National branches continue to be protected by State National's old charter once State National had been merged out of existence, its charter eliminated?

Baker, Central's lawyer, thought so. There was also a law on the books in Alabama (Title 5, Section 170 of the 1940 Code of Alabama), which was passed in 1919, in the face of the 1911 bill, that read:

> Any bank or trust company doing a banking business may consolidate or merge with or transfer its assets and liabilities to another bank or trust company, and any trust company doing a banking business may move its office or place of business from one city or town to another city or town within the state.

Moreover, Title 10 of the State Code stated that in a merger the surviving corporation is entitled to "every right, privilege and thing of value" that either corporation possessed before the merger. While branching was proscribed, bank mergers were recognized in Alabama law and had routinely occurred, although only State National had crossed county lines in its mergers. It was even stipulated that banks could merge only with other banks. What Central was attempting, if not clearly legal, was at least defensible.

Local-option laws dictated that the headquarters of the merged bank be in Birmingham. The law for Jefferson County was written in such a way that only banks headquartered there could branch in the county. If the headquarters had been established in Decatur, Central would likely have been frozen at five branches in Jefferson County. The law in Morgan County, where Decatur is located, was not similarly restrictive.

Brock and his associates had to choose between two different methods they could use to combine State National and Central. They could make both banks members of Alabama's first multibank holding company, the arrangement the Morrows had evidently been exploring with State National. The stock would all be exchanged for holding company stock, leaving one set of shareholders owning both banks and the umbrella corporation. But the two banks would remain banks, with separate boards of directors, charters, capital accounts, lending limits, branches and regulatory examinations. Central could still expand statewide by acquiring banks in chosen markets, but the acquisitions would have to be operated as affiliate banks instead of branches.

The holding company would have been the safer route to take. Although the pioneer who tried to form the first multibank holding company in Alabama could expect to meet opposition from unit bank supporters, as Frank Plummer was shortly to find out, the silence of Alabama law on the subject of multibank holding companies made them likely to survive any legal challenge. A holding company would not depend on Central's ability to bring State National's grandfathered branching privileges safely through a merger. Moreover, the holding company could make acquisitions more palatably: local directors and officers would keep their titles; the idea that the bank had passed into alien hands would be lessened. In retrospect, the holding company would have been the right choice, the one that would work.

But the Central group took the riskier, more radical option of trying to merge the two banks into a single bank, under Central's charter. Brock remembers seeking advice from Bank of Virginia's Rick Deane and New York investment banker Harry Keefe as to which form was preferable and being advised to seek the merger. The merger, by eliminating duplication, would come to be regarded by most bankers as more efficient and economical than the holding company. It would also allow more centralized management and greater control over the system and assure Central of one day becoming the biggest bank in Alabama. So Brock decided to go for the gold. It was one of the few strategic mistakes he would make.

Once control of State National was secure and Brock had determined to merge the banks under Central's charter, he notified the state superintendent of banking, C. E. Avinger. Avinger, a former running back with the New York Giants, knew what an angry, swarming defense could do to a fellow, so he decided to pick up a blocker. He referred the matter to Attorney General MacDonald Gallion for a legal opinion. Gallion came back, on September 30, 1968, with his finding that Central and State National could be merged without violating state or federal law, that the merged bank could continue to operate all existing branches, and that Central would be permitted to establish new branches in Jefferson County. It was just what Central wanted to hear.

But the opposing bankers, who were talking and putting together a strategy to block the merger, put enough heat on Avinger that he agreed to ask the attorney general's office to reconsider its opinion. The second opinion, this time issued over the signature of Assistant Attorney General David W. Clark, reaffirmed the first one, and Avinger announced that he would have no choice but to approve the merger. Clark's opinion noted that "the Attorney General's opinions are advisory in nature. Such opinion does not deny any aggrieved party the right to have the matter determined by a court." The Central crowd had reason to suspect that an aggrieved party of Alabama bankers would seek their day in court.

The opposition party was organizing and quickly growing. An October 15, 1968, story in the Birmingham *News* reported that seven banks had organized to block the Central/State National merger: John Hand's First National of Birmingham, Jim Simpson's Exchange Security, the Morrows' City National of Birmingham, BTNB, Union Bank & Trust of Montgomery and two Selma banks. An update the following day expanded the number to 16, and listed First National of Scottsboro, J. C. Jacobs Banking Co. of Scottsboro, First National of Florence, Merchants National of Mobile, First National of Dothan, First National of Ashford, and First National of Jasper. By October 30, the papers reported that 107 Alabama banks were petitioning Avinger to stop the merger. They were being represented by Exchange Security's law firm, Lange, Simpson, Robinson & Somerville, and Simpson himself was directing the campaign. The Lange Simpson offices were becoming the command headquarters for the block-Brock effort.

◇

In early January of 1969, according to depositions taken in subsequent litigation, William Ellis, a Birmingham attorney who practiced law by himself, returned to his office in the First National Bank building after taking care of some business at the Courthouse and found a message that John Hand wanted to talk to him. Ellis knew Hand from the Birmingham Country Club. First National's law firm, Cabaniss, Johnston, Gardner

& Clark, had asked Ellis to undertake certain investigations into the Central/State National merger the preceding August and paid him for his work. Ellis owed First National approximately $16,500 at the time he got Hand's message. More to the point, he had also owned for more than 12 years 532 shares of stock in State National Bank.

Later that afternoon, Ellis dropped by the bank to see Hand, who asked if Ellis still owned his State National stock. When Ellis said that he did, Hand told him, in Ellis' words, "You know that Jim Simpson, or his firm, . . . were looking into it . . . representing some banks . . . and that if I was interested I might talk to him . . . He said just go on up there if you want to; you might talk to them because they're representing the bankers on this."

Ellis had something the Alabama banks lacked, something attorneys call "standing." While other banks might be dismissed as disgruntled competitors, Ellis could claim that he was being injured as a State National shareholder. On January 10, the lawsuit to stop the merger was filed: *William H. Ellis v. State National Bank of Alabama, et al.* For good measure, a second suit was filed ten days later on essentially the same issues, this one with banks as plaintiffs: *The American National Bank of Gadsden, et al v. Central Bank & Trust Company, et al.*

The lines were being drawn for a major showdown in court, and both sides moved to bolster their legal staffs. Simpson, now in his late 70s, relied heavily on two young members of his firm, Robert McDavid Smith and William G. Somerville. Most of the banks who participated in the suit had their own attorneys, who would offer suggestions, Smith recalls. Once the battle to block the merger went beyond the attorney general and superintendent of banking and entered the litigation phase, the number of formal plaintiffs dropped to a relatively few banks, mostly from Birmingham and north Alabama, markets where Central and State National were strongest, Smith explains. Ellis came along at the last minute and was chosen to be the nominal plaintiff because of his shareholder standing.

Baker knew he would need heavier artillery for this case than his own small law firm could provide, so he called his old friend Eason Balch, a partner in the larger Birmingham law firm Martin, Balch, Bingham, Hawthorne & Williams. Lew Odom, an aide to Sen. John Sparkman and, prior to August 1968, the general counsel of the Senate Banking Committee in Washington, was also consulted.

Because so many of the major banks in northern Alabama were involved in the suit, it was difficult to find a judge who was not connected in some way to one of the parties. All three judges for the U.S. District Court for north Alabama excused themselves, and Judge Daniel H. Thomas from the southern Alabama district was assigned the case. When a Mobile judge was designated, Central retained the prominent Mobile law firm Lyon, Pipes & Cook to represent it as well. Baker took an active role, and the Harrises from Decatur were also used, but the man who emerged as Central's principal legal strategist and workhorse was a tenacious young attorney from Martin, Balch, Bingham named James Hancock. Hancock was excited by the implications of the case and immersed himself in the details. He went on to become Central's primary counsel until his appointment to the federal bench in 1973. The long proceedings would throw Baker together with Martin, Balch, Bingham attorneys so much that, before it was over, he left his former law firm to join what became Balch, Bingham, Baker, Hawthorne, Williams & Ward.

The Ellis suit pretty much threw the book at the merging banks. It charged them with violating the federal Clayton Antitrust Act, potentially damaging to shareholder Ellis because Clayton violations were punishable by forced divestiture and payment of treble damages to competing banks. Most of the complaint focused on Alabama branching law and held that the merger would violate the 1911 anti-branching law; that Central would have no legal basis for keeping branches grandfathered to State National once State National was erased by the merger; that the right to move branches is not established by law, and that Central would violate the local-option bill allowing branching in Jefferson County by acquiring branches in other counties.

In addition, there were some fairly technical arguments, added almost as an afterthought by the lawyers, as Somerville recalls, that dealt with whether Alabama law met the requirements of federal law for a national bank to merge into a state bank.

In April, additional charges were filed, claiming that the merger violated federal securities requirements, specifically the Williams Act. These charges particularly troubled the Central team. The Williams Act had been signed into law by President Lyndon Johnson on July 29, 1968, just as Central was wrapping up its acquisition of 40 percent of the State National stock. "We were particularly worried about the Williams Act and knew the minute LBJ signed it," Brock recalls. "We knew we had to make all our purchases before the bill was signed, but we slipped up somehow and some of the stock was bought by mistake just after the Williams Act was signed, which put us in violation." The Williams Act, designed to protect firms from unfriendly takeovers, required investors to disclose their actions if they acquired more than 10 percent of a target company's stock. In one of the early judgments involving a Williams Act violation, the shares obtained by a violator were neutralized and lost their voting power. If such a judgment were applied to Central, the whole takeover could have been overturned.

On its branching issues, the lawsuit had the potential to become a landmark case for banking structure in Alabama. If Central's contention held — that the 1911 act forbade establishment of new branches but that other laws specifically allowed banks to merge across county lines, retain branches and move them at will — the 1911 law would be rendered largely irrelevant. Other banks would necessarily follow Central's example, and mergers would build statewide systems at the expense of local control. It would overturn the law most bankers thought they were operating under. Considerable interest focused on the proceedings.

The merger was an accomplished fact if three hurdles could be passed: a two-thirds vote for merger by shareholders of the two organizations; approval by the Alabama banking superintendent, and approval by the FDIC. The lawsuits asked the judge to enjoin Avinger and the FDIC from approving Central's application and to issue an injunction stopping the shareholder meetings, which were scheduled for January 28. On January 24, Judge Thomas denied the injunction to stop the meetings but instructed Avinger and the FDIC to take no action until the court had ruled on the issues of the case. Central had won the first round in court, and the shareholder meetings were held as scheduled.

Ellis, who was regarded by the Central team as a pawn of the big Birmingham banks but sincere in his opposition to the merger, appeared at the State National shareholder meeting and pleaded with shareholders to reject the merger. He opened by reflecting that State National had done very well in its recent history and congratulated her officers. He had filed suit to block the merger, he explained, because its legality was doubtful and placed State National's powers in jeopardy. "Remember, please, State National is not taking over Central; Central is taking over State National. State National has a right under the grandfather clause of the Alabama law to keep branches; Central does not have that right under that law, for it was not even a bank until over 50 years after the grandfather clause was made law — back in 1911," he noted.

> And let us not deceive ourselves. All those issues will be raised and, in my judgement, will be fought as hard as the banks contesting the merger can fight. . . . In that suit they are claiming that the proposed merger violates the Clayton Act regulating restraint of trade; they are claiming that the proposed merger will cause us at State National to lose all our branches on the theory that such a right cannot be transferred to another bank, and they have legal authority which indicates that they may be right. . . .
>
> I am not unmindful of the fact that some good legal minds have said that the proposed merger is completely legal. However, I also know that other good legal minds have given opinions to the contesting banks that the merger is both illegal and will cause State National's branches to be lost. As a lawyer of over 40 years' experience, I do not like to guess the outcome of a case with such good legal minds on both sides. However, one of those groups of good legal minds is bound to be wrong. The risk to a stockholder is just too great to take, in my mind, by voting on a merger so fraught with unanswered and serious questions.
>
> . . . I cannot work up much enthusiasm to aid a band which has been in existence only five years in swallowing State National with three quarters of a century of service to North Alabama. I cannot work up much enthusiasm to aid a Bir-

> mingham bank with six banking offices to swallow State National with 25 banking offices, especially when the swallowing could cause the loss of those 25. I cannot work up much enthusiasm to aid a bank with some 80 million dollars in resources in swallowing up State National with some 211 millions of dollars of resources. I cannot work up much enthusiasm to assist a bank way down the line to swallow State National, now Alabama's third largest bank.
>
> The merger of State National into Central of Birmingham under its charter and name, with the loss of State National's charter, its name and its headquarters in North Alabama is too much like the bait swallowing the fish, as I see it.

It was an eloquent but futile plea. State National shareholders voted 295,642 - 20,289 in favor of the merger, although those attending the meeting in person did vote 6,200 - 5,396 against merger. While Central controlled only 40 percent of the State National stock, 84 percent had voted for merger, despite the legal cloud. Round two had gone to Brock. He was making headway with his idea that State National could do even better than it had been doing, that the merger would create a powerful bank that would please shareholders of both institutions. The Central shareholders, as expected, ratified the merger overwhelmingly: 756,219 - 858.

The merger was still blocked, however, because Judge Thomas had ordered Avinger and the FDIC to take no action until the court ruled. The nonjury trial began before Judge Thomas in Birmingham on June 2, 1969. Although the case would generate reams of written material, the trial itself took less than two days and was a rather simple procedure. Because the two sides essentially agreed on the facts of the case but disagreed on the application of relevant laws, both sides agreed to a stipulation of the facts. Therefore, the trial began with the material facts already agreed upon, making testimony unnecessary. Judge Thomas further simplified the procedure by accepting Central's motion to consolidate the two suits *(Ellis v. State National* and *American National v. Central)* for trial.

Sam Pipes of the Mobile law firm argued most of Central's case at the trial. Simpson himself gave the plaintiff's summation, pleading fervently that the state's system of independent community banks should not be compromised by allowing aggressive expansion. The judge closed the trial after several hours of legal arguments had been heard and went off to think about his verdict.

In rendering his decision on June 17, Judge Thomas divided the issues into two questions: Is the merger legally permissible under state and federal law? May the surviving bank operate all of the branches of both banks? Only if the merger was found to be legal would the status of branches and branching rights be considered. As it turned out, no decision would ever be made on the substantial issues raised by the case. Judge Thomas based his ruling on a technicality in one of the minor issues raised by the plaintiffs: the permissibility of a national bank merging into a state bank. Basing the decision on such narrow grounds may have been a strategic choice. In a February 7, 1969, letter to Hancock, Paul E. d'Hedouville, a Washington attorney representing the FDIC, noted, "It is my understanding that the Court seems to be looking for a reasonable way to avoid a decision on the merits."

State and national banks had merged in Alabama without legal challenge. The Bank for Savings was a state bank that merged into one of the banks bringing the lawsuit, Birmingham Trust National Bank, back in 1963, and a state bank in Madison had merged in 1968 with another of the plaintiffs, the First National Bank of Huntsville. The national banks were the survivors in these cases, however. Federal law permitted national banks to convert into, merge or consolidate with state banks only if "under the law of the State in which the national bank is located, State banks may without approval of any State authority convert into and merge or consolidate with, national banking associations under limitations or conditions no more restrictive than those contained in Section 214a of this Title." (12 U.S.C.A. 214c) It is essentially a reciprocity test. State law must be no more restrictive than federal law if a national bank is allowed to merge into a state bank.

Since federal law permitted mergers of state and national banks only if "State banks may without approval of any State authority convert into and merge or consolidate with, national banking associations," the decision hinged on whether the approval of the state banking superintendent was required.

Now Central had pointed out that under Sections 181-184 of Title 5 of the Alabama Code, state banks were allowed to "convert into or consolidate" with national banks without the superintendent's approval, but the judge ruled that this was still not enough. He emphasized the words "convert into and merge or consolidate" to interpret the federal law as specifying three separate legal operations: conversion, merger and consolidation. He literally transformed the "or" into an "and" when he concluded that "unless a State bank can convert into, merge with *and* consolidate with a national bank without State approval, then a national bank cannot convert into, merge with and consolidate with a State bank." (Italics added.) Since the state law only waived the superintendent's approval in two cases, conversion or consolidation, the superintendent's approval was construed by the judge as necessary for the third situation, merger. This made the state law more restrictive than the federal law and made the merger of State National into Central illegal.

Judge Thomas ordered the banks not to merge, Avinger and the FDIC not to approve any merger. At Central's request, the judge, while issuing a technical correction to his decision, added that his decision had no bearing on the question of whether branches could be retained if the merger were ever ruled to be permissible.

The decision still exasperates Hancock. "We did not deserve to lose the case on the grounds on which we lost it, on what appeared to be sham grounds. That decision required reading a disjunctive 'or' as a conjunctive 'and.' We did deserve to lose on the basis of securities violations, Williams Act violations. That law required reports to the target company in a takeover, and Central had violated that act, accidentally, in a lot of ways. But we should not have lost it as we did. We did not lose the case on the law; we lost it on the politics. I'm a member of the federal judiciary now myself, but judges are not always as independent as they should be, and this was one of those times," Hancock charges. From the perspective of the plaintiffs, attorney Somerville smiles and declines to dispute claims that the decision was based on a rather tortured reading of an almost incidental technicality.

But the decision was rendered, and Central had lost. Losing was a novelty. The bank had never lost on any matter of such importance. They were not likely to lose again, the Central group decided, so on July 15, Central appealed the case to the U.S. Court of Appeals, Fifth Circuit. Brock and Nelson announced the appeal to the press, publicly expressing confidence that they would win the case on appeal. That show of solidarity was a desperate charade. Behind the scenes, the merger agreement was falling apart. The State National board had virtually decided to cancel it. On June 19, two days after Judge Thomas' decision, the two bank boards met jointly in Decatur. Nelson argued that no appeal should be filed and that the merger should be abandoned, citing mounting legal fees, deteriorating morale among State National officers and legislative reprisals against State National. The State National board was solidly behind Nelson this time. Brock produced Balch, who said the chances of winning an appeal were good. Balch also pointed out that the appeal could be dropped later, and he offered to waive his legal fees for State National. Struggling to buy time, Brock urged a special meeting to poll shareholders.

All Brock could get was a tentative show of support for preserving the merger agreement and pursuing the appeal. The tension continued. After an upset Brock complained about persistent rumors that State National was abandoning the merger, Wyker, in an August 5 letter to Brock, promised no surprise moves but reiterated the board's "intent to withdraw from the merger." The State National directors were not necessarily opposed to affiliation, but they now clearly preferred Nelson's favorite, the multibank holding company.

At the December 9, 1969, meeting of the State National board, the issue was finally resolved. A resolution was introduced by Nelson, seconded by Agricola and passed by the board. It acknowledged that the board had considered "the advisability of withdrawing from and terminating said Merger Agreement," and concluded after careful consideration that it was in the best interest of State National to enter a holding company with Central rather than consummate the merger. The resolution supported the appeal of the Thomas decision, however, because that judgment "is a precedent which may and probably will be injurious to State National and should be overturned." The merger agreement should remain an option, the resolution said, in case a holding company could not be formed. The directors went on record as saying "that while the Merger Agreement should not be abandoned or terminated at the present time, it will probably be abandoned and terminated even in the event of a favorable decision in the appeal now pending . . . and that in lieu of said Merger Agreement being consummated the two banks will likely procure the formation of a holding company for the holding of the stock in the two banks. . . . " Brock kept the appeal alive, but prospects for a merger were fading.

The first court decision moved relatively quickly in 1968 from the January 10 filing to the June 2 trial and June 17 decision. The appeal process dragged on until October 28, 1970, when a three-judge panel of the U.S. Court of Appeals, meeting in New Orleans, upheld the decision by Judge Thomas. Central had lost again.

Still Brock would not give up, although legal costs were mounting and support was shifting strongly to formation of a holding company. The case was appealed again, this time to the U.S. Supreme Court. It was July 27, 1971, when Central went down for the third and final time. The Supreme Court refused to hear the case. The merger was blocked. The chance to be the biggest bank in Alabama was lost. Only the holding company option now remained, and that option had narrowly survived an all-out effort by most of the banks in Alabama to shut every door by which Central could expand outside of Birmingham.

SHAKE HANDS WITH "RED"—A PAN-AM BOY FROM GADSDEN, WHO IS GOING PLACES

Everyone up around Gadsden, Alabama, knows "Red".

"Red" is the sixteen year old son of Harry B. Brock, PAN-AM distributor at Gadsden. He is typical of the youngsters in the PAN-AM Family, and his latest exploits are told as follows by his father:

"Until this spring Red had charge of the livestock on my country place in Etowah County. However, he wanted to get into the war effort in some way or other during vacation period from the Tennessee Miltary Academy where he is now a junior. So one afternoon he went down to see some engineers who had come to Gadsden to build a new chemical war plant. By pushing his way in he got a promise of a job at 7 o'clock Monday morning. He reported in full soldier's uniform and his first job was to go with a captain to Talladega to get a new station wagon. He drove the engineers over the field for a couple of days and then the general manager brought "Red" into Headquarters and gave him a desk job in the front office. He helped them fill out their application cards. Finally his boss told him to use his own judgment in selecting the men and "Red" met all applicants for jobs and hired 11 truck drivers and several linemen. He is the only local man this firm hired in the office. You ought to see him sitting at his desk in a big swivel chair. I went in to see him and he told me there were 7 men ahead so I would have to line up and take my turn. He hated to leave his job, but he had to get back to school."

"Red" Brock

Mr. Brock didn't point out that even while he was on his new job, "Red" found time before and after office hours to look after his cows, pigs, horses, and chickens.

An October 1942 article from Harry B. Brock, Sr.'s, company newspaper The Panorama. *Mr. Brock was the Gadsden, Alabama, distributor for the New Orleans-based Pan-Am oil company.*

Harry Brock at Tennessee Military Institute. Senior year, 1943.

Opening Day, March 2, 1964

Governor George Wallace and Harry Brock cutting the ribbon for Central Bank and Trust Company's first office on First Avenue North in Birmingham.

George Wallace, Governor of Alabama, talking with John Hand, President of the First National Bank of Birmingham. "If you want to see me, John, you'll have to come here." And he came. Listening is U.S. Senator from Alabama, Jim Allen.

Lobby of Central Bank's first office on First Avenue North during opening week, 1964.

Lloyd Rains (left) with customer Frank Lynch at Central Bank's first office on First Avenue North. Rains, Central's first vice-president, was a cautious lender and a soft-spoken, even-tempered man – a good foil to Harry Brock. Together they would lead Central through its formative years.

First Stockholders Meeting at First Avenue North. March, 1965.

Founders, Central Bank and Trust Company, 1964
Seated: Harry B. Brock, Jr., Schuyler A. Baker. Standing (l-r): Frank L. Hardy, John R. Israel, Jr., R. Hugh Daniel, Dr. Wendell H. Taylor, Stewart H. Welch, Jr.

Twenty years after the opening of the original headquarters (right), 1987 marks the arrival of Central's new Administrative Headquarters Building on the Birmingham Southside. This will be the electronic nerve center of the entire organization.

Central Bank's new headquarters building, located at the corner of 20th Street and Seventh Avenue South adjacent to the UAB medical complex, opened for business in October, 1967.

R. Hugh Daniel and Harry B. Brock, Jr., two of the Central players in A Competitive Spirit.

CHAPTER SIX

Shootout In Montgomery

THE LAWSUIT WAS PART of a two-pronged counterattack by the Alabama bankers and barely half of the problem Central faced in 1969. The bankers were unwilling to trust to anything as unpredictable as a federal court. They wanted to be certain that the overbearing ambition of Central was blocked before one rogue bank upset the whole banking system of Alabama. If what Brock was trying to do was not already illegal, it would be by the time they finished with the legislature in Montgomery. Though Brock had chosen to pursue a merger, his bold, expansionary move heightened anxiety over the potential for large urban banks to expand across the state with multibank holding companies. A substantial number of angry, apprehensive bankers were good and ready to slam some doors, bolt them shut and then nail boards over them to prevent an upheaval in the banking structure of Alabama.

The issue came to a head on January 15 just five days after Central had been slapped with the first lawsuit, when the executive committee of the Alabama Bankers Association met in Montgomery. The meeting, ironically, was chaired by Nelson as president of AlaBA. Newton DeBardeleben, John Hand's aide-de-camp at the First National Bank of Birmingham, presented a resolution that called for legislation to accomplish three things: ban multibank holding companies from Alabama, freeze State National in its present locations, and clarify branching law so that mergers clearly fell under the 1911 branching ban.

Brock asked for and was granted permission to address the committee. Knowing well that the power in AlaBA lay with the small community banks, Brock portrayed his opposition as coming from the big Birmingham banks who were trying to squelch competition in order to maintain their dominance. The large banks, he charged, had pressured small banks to oppose Central by threatening to expand statewide if Central did, trying to force the community banks to stop Central in order to avoid open statewide branching. Central, he countered, was the small banks' friend and had initiated many correspondent services to aid small banks.

"It should be obvious that we did not, and are not now, promoting statewide branching," Brock insisted. "In fact, to do so would undermine the large premium which the investors paid for stock in a bank that historically had the right to operate limited branches in other counties," he claimed, although he also acknowledged that "attorneys for the two banks, while researching the law, reported to management that, in their opinion, any two banks in Alabama could merge, and that State National Bank, in fact, did not have an exclusive franchise."

If clarification of branching law was in order through new legislation, he appealed to their sense of "fair play" to continue State National's grandfathered protection from any new restrictions. The large banks had never challenged State National's branching rights before, he pointed out, and he charged them with hypocrisy for doing so at that time: "We might suggest that one reason the Birmingham banks have never opposed State National Bank before is because each one of them had visions that they themselves might be able to merge with this bank which had valuable 'grandfather privileges.' In fact, more than one of these large banks in Birmingham has approached officials of State National Bank in the past about merging. . . . We do not think that the large banks are fighting with clean hands," Brock protested. "They are not fighting for the small banks. They are fighting new competition for themselves."

He capitalized on Central's underdog status to attack the monopoly charges. "The large banks in Jefferson County say in their petition that we will create a monopoly. This charge is obviously ridiculous because two banks in Birmingham now have 77 percent of the commercial bank deposits in that city and some 22 percent of the commercial bank deposits in the entire state. . . . Incidentally, Central Bank, the so-called monopoly bank, has presently less than 2 percent of the commercial deposits in the State of Alabama. Who has the monopoly? Let the figures speak for themselves!"

It was a rousing if not altogether consistent defense, but it left Brock where he started — on the short end of a 13-2 vote by the executive committee. When Nelson moved to refer the matter to the full AlaBA membership, his motion died for lack of a second. Brock was unable then, or in subsequent efforts, to drive a wedge between the large and small banks opposing him, and small banks in Alabama, with a few scattered exceptions, remained fiercely opposed to Central's efforts to expand. Eighteen years later, Brock has made his peace with most of his big-bank opponents but is still considered the enemy by some community bankers in Alabama.

Brock expected to lose his case in the courts of AlaBA. Even the effort to refer the decision to the full AlaBA membership was more a bid to buy time than an effort to defeat the resolution, Brock acknowledges. The issue was escalating. It was no longer a banking issue; it was becoming a public issue, and Central's campaign would be for public understanding and approval. The vote Central absolutely had to win was not in AlaBA but in the state legislature in Montgomery.

As the winds of war were swirling, Brock, at a cocktail party, heard about Harry Bandouveris from Norma Seibels, a Central teller who was also the wife of Birmingham Mayor George G. Seibels. Bandouveris was a savvy political campaigner and public relations consultant from Arizona who had worked in the Goldwater presidential campaign of 1964 and then in 1967 successfully helped to elect Seibels as Birmingham's first Republican mayor in decades. Bandouveris had recently moved to Birmingham and was available, so Brock enlisted his aid. In Bandouveris' first report to Brock, he presented a campaign depicting Central as an octopus with tentacles reaching ominously all over Alabama. Brock was startled. He remembers, with a chuckle, Bandouveris saying, "This is the campaign I'll sell to John Hand if you don't hire me to work for your side." Bandouveris simply recalls that he was following his standard strategy of anticipating how the other side would attack and fashioning a good defense against it.

The defense would ridicule the notion that Central constituted a monopolistic threat. To this end, Bandouveris developed a series of cartoons using a football theme. The big banks appeared in the cartoons as huge, hulking Number 77, representing their 77-percent market share in Birmingham, while Central appeared as scrappy, little Number 6. Number 77 was always howling, like a tearful mama's boy, about how Number 6 was playing too rough and taking advantage of him. Central ran the cartoons in newspapers and sent printed copies to opinion leaders in Alabama, including most members of the legislature. The campaign caught people's attention and created conversation and a few chuckles. The cartoons may have undercut efforts by the other side to raise public concern about the Central menace, but they did not turn back an opposition which was powerful, organized, well-funded, determined, and growing daily during the winter and spring of 1969.

Brock had bought prominent legal help for Central's lawsuits and hired a slick PR gun to help influence public opinion, but he did not hire a lobbyist to lead the all-important fight in the legislature in Montgomery. That was one job he figured, despite his inexperience, he had better do for himself.

As spring wore on and the 1969 legislative session approached, AlaBA had its outside general counsel, Robert E. Steiner III of the prominent Montgomery firm of Steiner, Crum and Baker, draft a bill for introduction, and, on May 20, 1969, when the General Assembly convened, House Bill 218 and Senate Bill 245 were introduced. The two bills were identical versions of the AlaBA-Steiner bill, a short, simple and potentially decisive piece of legislation. It reaffirmed the 1911 law forbidding any kind of banking office other than the home (headquarters) office unless local-option legislation permitted countywide branching. It forbade establishing "branch banks or other offices" across county lines "whether said branch is newly opened or acquired by merger, consolidation or otherwise." If passed, the 1969 law would clearly make mergers subject to the 1911 branching restrictions.

A second section of the bill reaffirmed local-option branching authorization but limited the effects of such laws to the "corporate limits of the municipalities within the geographical confines of the county" in which the bank is headquartered.

A third section apparently would have invalidated State National's branching system. It provided that, aside from local-option exceptions, "no bank having its principal place of business in Alabama may establish or operate any branch in any county other than that of the principal place of business of such bank, whether by merger, consolidation, opening a new branch, moving an existing branch or otherwise." No grandfathered exceptions were recognized. At the very least, this section would have prevented further branch moves by State National, whether or not it merged with Central.

The fourth section struck at the heart of the Central-State National merger:

> Should any two or more banks operating in Alabama merge or consolidate or should any bank acquire by lease or by purchase either the stock or controlling interest in the stock or all or substantially all of the assets of any other bank operating in Alabama, then in either event, no branch bank may thereafter be owned or operated except in the county of the principal place of business of only the surviving bank. To this end, the Directors by resolution shall on or before such merger, consolidation or acquisition elect the county in which the surviving bank shall operate and immediately close the branch or branches in all other counties and thereafter as promptly as possible dispose of such real property.

Central, if it merged with State National, could retain none of State National's offices, not even the Decatur headquarters, under this proposed law. It would have destroyed any incentive to merge.

A fifth section recognized one-bank holding companies but made it illegal "for any holding company in Alabama to own or control two or more banks in Alabama." The bill would take effect immediately on passage and signature by the governor and would repeal all earlier laws inconsistent with it. It was apparently iron-clad ratification of what most bankers had considered the banking law of Alabama since 1911. Statewide or even cross-county banking organizations would not be permitted. Central would have no foreseeable way to expand beyond Jefferson County. "We had to defeat that bill," Brock observes. "It would have blocked everything we were trying to do."

The full weight of the Alabama Bankers Association was behind the bill, and the Alabama Bankers Association in 1969 was a potent lobbying force, perhaps the strongest in the state. AlaBA's executive director Howard Morris had been rallying his well-organized troops ever since January when a memo stated, "It is necessary for those of us opposed to branching across county lines to begin to work promptly and vigorously to explain our thoughts and desires to our legislators." It asked the "Minuteman" banker "to contact your legislator and ask for his support. . . ." The Minutemen were local bankers responsible for making the political contacts that were often the most effective. Each legislator had a Minuteman banker contact, someone he knew well from his home district, often his own banker, who would contact him to let him know what the Alabama bankers wanted on legislation pertaining to banking.

When the AlaBA bills were introduced, House Speaker Rankin Fite assigned the bill to the State Administration Committee, chaired by Drexel Cook of Luverne. State Senate President Joe Goodwyn, in his chamber, assigned the bill to the Senate Banking Committee, chaired by Jimmy Clark of Eufaula. The battle was on.

Much of the responsibility for getting the bill passed in the House fell to Charles Snell. Snell was a country banker, president of the Citizens Bank of Shawmut. He had also been a member of the Alabama House since 1962. Snell was a savvy member of both the AlaBA and the legislative establishments, a man with lots of friends in the right places and a solid knowledge of how to get things done in the legislature. He made sure that House members had heard from their Minuteman bankers; then Snell canvassed his colleagues. He found that 76 of the 105 House members promised to vote in favor of the bill, he recalls — a comfortable majority. So he kept up contact with his colleagues, making sure he didn't lose any votes and trying to persuade others to join the cause. And he waited for the vote he felt sure he was ready for.

The Alabama Bankers' Minutemen kept up their contact

with legislators, too. AlaBA, under the banner of the "Hometown Bankers," maintained a hospitality suite in the Holiday Inn, four blocks from the capitol. Legislators were always welcome, throughout the three-month session, to drop by for a free drink and a little friendly persuasion. Many did. Since Central was a dues-paying member of AlaBA, Brock would sometimes drop by the suite himself and get in his licks with the legislators, explaining his opposition to AlaBA.

Snell began to worry about the wait as the summer went by. He kept checking with his old friend Cook to see when the bill would receive attention from Cook's committee, but Cook would only shake his head and give Snell no information. The State Administration Committee was not an improper place to assign the bill, according to Snell, because there was no House Banking Committee at that time, but the State Administration Committee had a special function in 1969 which Snell was beginning to understand and which would spell trouble for him. It was becoming known as the speaker's committee, a cooperative place to which the speaker could refer bills he wanted to be certain to control. If the speaker wanted a particular bill to die on the vine, he would assign it to State Administration, where his close ally Cook would keep it bottled up indefinitely; that, Snell found, was exactly what was happening. State Administration, in 1969, would earn its reputation as the "graveyard committee." To insure that it took no action, the committee never formally met during the 1969 session. Progress was not much greater in the Senate, where Clark deferred action on the bill until the House acted first.

Things, Brock noted with satisfaction, were progressing according to plan. Brock was a planner. According to his wife, he always had a strategic plan, then a contingency plan in case the master plan went awry, and sometimes a third plan in case the first two both miscarried. He had anticipated, even before he carried out his takeover of State National, that opponents might try to stop him in the legislature. One of his top priorities, well before AlaBA even began to prepare legislation, was to talk with legislative leaders and key committee members and secure their promises not to change the law, he recalls. They agreed.

As the battle in Montgomery shaped up, Central prepared file cards on legislators, identifying a primary group of lawmakers — members of the committees to which the bill had been assigned, the people whose support Central would need to keep the bills from seeing action or perhaps to defeat them if they ever came up for a committee vote. Then there was a secondary group of legislators who were known to have influence on the primary group. Finally, there were all the other members of the legislature whose votes would matter if the strategic plan misfired and the bills came up for a vote from the full House or Senate.

The governor was a political factor that was difficult to assess. Central no longer had a friendly Wallace in the governor's mansion. Lurleen Wallace, elected as a surrogate when her husband was blocked by the Alabama constitution from succeeding himself, died of cancer on May 7, 1968. The new governor was Albert Brewer, and so closely had Wallace exercised political power while he or his wife was governor that no one knew exactly what Brewer stood for or how much and in what ways he would exercise the power of the governor's office. Brewer was not considered a Wallace man. But he was a north Alabama man — from Decatur, in fact — and a founding director of an independent bank there. Both Brock and the State National directors were acquainted with him. Brock paid a visit to Brewer and, by his recollection, got no promise of support from Brewer but an agreement that Brewer would stay out of the fight and leave the matter up to the legislature.

Brewer, personally skeptical about the benefits of branch banking, was scheduled to address the AlaBA convention in April 1969 — at a time when the issue was heating up and the lobbying had already begun, although the legislature was not yet in session. In his remarks, Brewer stated, "In my opinion, branch banking is not in the best interests of this state. If we are going to abolish branch banking in Alabama, we will not close the front door and leave the back door open. I'm talking about holding companies. It is just a question of wearing a black hat instead of a white hat. However, I will do what the legislature directs."

"BREWER BLASTS BRANCH BANKING," the Birmingham *Post-Herald* proclaimed in its headlines over the story of Brewer's speech. "GOVERNOR SUPPORTS SMALL BANKS," declared the Montgomery *Advertiser*. According to the lead in the Birmingham *News*, "Gov. Albert Brewer has backed small-town banking interests in supporting present laws against branch banking." Perhaps more emphasis should have been given to Brewer's last sentence. Brock did have the neutrality commitment he needed from Brewer. Brock contacted Brewer after the speech and, in an April 18th letter, reminded the governor of their quiet understanding: "Since my first conversation with you last summer about our plan we have always been careful not to quote your commitment at that time." Later, Morris would bemoan, "Governor Brewer, while apparently philosophically opposed to branch banking, was either unable or unwilling to give the bill the help it needed in the face of such implacable and powerful opposition."

"Implacable" and "powerful" would be odd words for the nearly united banking establishment of Alabama to use to describe one middle-sized, isolated bank and its still-uneasy bride-to-be, but Morris, Snell and the AlaBA were finding that they faced an unexpected juggernaut that was indeed powerful and implacable. Central was proving to be a tough adversary. Brock, by all accounts, was a very effective lobbyist in behalf of his cause. "Harry Brock was intelligent and caught on to the ways of the legislature much more rapidly than people thought he would," Morris admits. "He was able to break down some of the contacts we assumed were solidly for us." And Brock was working hard, even when he seemed to have the bills securely bottled up. "You have to help your friends — take some of the heat off them by fighting for your own cause aggressively and keeping the other side worried," Brock explains. Brock and often Clyde Tate from Central were busy in Montgomery almost every day the legislature or the all-important committees were meeting. Snell recalls making his rounds and lobbying key legislators who would tell him that Brock had been by shortly before.

The fact that Brock, a bank president, was doing his own lobbying helped Central a lot. The legislators were flattered when the head man came calling instead of sending a hired gun. It was virtually unheard of at that time for a bank president to come to Montgomery to call on legislators, except for some community bankers like Snell who were also legislators. Much of Brock's success was a matter of personal chemistry. Bankers generally regarded politics with some disdain and held themselves aloof from direct politicking. Laws, like sausages, are better not seen in the making, they agreed. Brock struck a strong rapport and sense of camaraderie with many lawmakers, the majority of whom represented rural districts. For all his considerable success as a Birmingham banker and his growing confidence and knowledge of how to wield power, Brock never moved far from his style as a good ol' country boy from Hokes Bluff. He was never busy or officious. He could put his arm around a man's shoulder and keep it there without making it seem strange. He could talk to a man, face to face, belly to belly, physical presence pressed against physical presence, without ever looking away or pulling back. He could be righteous: only asking for a fair chance to compete, to keep grandfathered rights long acknowledged by all parties. But he could also grin and wink, and show that he was a bit of a rascal, out to turn a situation to his advantage. He was consistently good-humored. He remembered everyone's name and his interests. He didn't take a friend for granted or write off a foe. He shrewdly played up his underdog status and his opposition from the big mules in Birmingham until he seemed like a good-hearted country boy seeking a more democratic marketplace and disturbing the feudal territories of the warlords of Birmingham.

The man who aspired to become the biggest Birmingham banker of them all got more mileage out of his anti-big-Birmingham-bank posture with the politicians in Montgomery than he ever did with the community bankers. A lot of the rural legislators shared Brock's resentment of the big banks' high-falutin ways. Many of them liked Brock, admired his feisty spirit, enjoyed his company and wished him well, even if they had philosophical reservations about branch banking. Brock developed so many friends among the legislators and became so adept at influencing opinions that his appearance on the floor of one of the chambers would cause a stir as lawmakers reached to shake his hand and say their word of welcome to good old Harry Brock. Legislative opponents would holler for the chair to clear the floor of visitors lest they lose more votes to Brock, some legislators recall.

Some members of the Central team were concerned about Brock. He was simultaneously running an innovative, fast-growing bank in Birmingham, struggling to hold together a still-touchy takeover in Decatur, supervising a legal campaign as he fought for his business plan in the federal courts, and carrying most of the weight of an intensive lobbying campaign in Montgomery. "We all knew Harry was under intense pressure and wished there were more we could do to help him," Jernigan recalls. But the truth was that Brock loved the excitement; the battles got his juices flowing and he thrived on the accumulated challenges. He particularly enjoyed the ruckus in Montgomery. Lowder groused a bit that Brock was spending too much time on politics, not enough time making profits in the banks. Gene Faulkner, president of a small bank in Prattville who became one of Central's regular political adversaries, observes, "I hate to go to the legislature and play the games they play there, but we have to look out for ourselves. Harry likes to fool with the legislature. He's down there almost every session."

Brock was fighting for his professional life, a fact that weighed more heavily on his wife than himself. Jane was indignant about the snubs and rumors and rejection coming from Alabama bankers, and frankly worried about the outcome. "We had personally borrowed a million dollars to invest in Harry's plan and here they were doing everything they could to destroy us," she recalls. But Harry, she says, would only smile and say he understood how his opponents felt, that he might say and do the same things if he were in their place. Life is too short for resentment; revenge wastes valuable time, he would tell Jane. He had a lot at stake, which certainly drove him onward, but at some point the thrill of the hunt itself took over and Brock, who would later hunt big game for pleasure, found himself enthralled to be playing a high-stakes game that suited his talents well.

Brock alone was a formidable lobbyist for Central's cause, but Brock alone was not what Howard Morris meant by "implacable" and "powerful." He probably had in mind Rankin

Fite, a rural legislator from Hamilton County in northwest Alabama. Already suffering noticeably from Parkinson's disease in 1969, Fite was serving what would be his last term as speaker. He left the legislature in 1973 and died in 1980. But in 1969 he was still near the height of his political power, which was impressive. Very little happened in the Alabama House without Fite's approval. Colleagues still speak of him with the kind of awe reserved for a legend. They say, "He was a masterful legislator." "He ruled the House." "He was very adept at using the legislative process to get what he wanted." And they regularly add things like, "He was vindictive as hell." If there was one vote in the Alabama House that counted more than all the other votes combined, it belonged to Rankin Fite, and Brock had Fite's vote. Cook recalls, "The speaker and I had an understanding that there was one specific time when that bill would be released from committee: when hell froze over."

Brock and Fite struck up an alliance that still puzzles observers of the Montgomery political scene. There was substantial curiosity as to why Fite took such a strong interest in blocking the stop-Brock bill. Fite generally kept his own counsel, and he carried his motives on this issue with him to the grave, but his colleagues speculate that Fite's own banking interests influenced his choice. Here Brock sheds some light on Fite's opposition to the bill. Fite was chairman, president and a major shareholder of the Marion County Banking Company. That bank also had an old charter (1905) and had operated a branch prior to 1911. Brock apparently convinced Fite that his bank, too, was entitled to claim branching privileges that would be destroyed by the AlaBA bill. Hancock, then Central's attorney, recalls helping Fite prepare legal filings to test his bank's branching rights. "Rankin Fite was always one to sniff out a good thing. I think Harry had convinced him that his bank could do something it probaby couldn't do," Hancock says.

If Fite was convinced that the AlaBA bill jeopardized his own banking interests as well as Brock's, it might well account for his powerful, implacable opposition to the bill. However, Fite was also giving AlaBA fits on its other big legislative cause in 1969 — the so-called "mini-code," which would have raised usury limits for banks and finance companies — so it is possible that Fite was feeling some unexplained animosity toward the association.

At any rate, Fite and Brock were working together, and Fite's legendary political influence had put the bankers' bill on ice. Morris was left to rail about "the most extraordinary display of a speaker's use of the chair's power to absolutely control the passage of all legislation." The speaker had a chair or two besides his own at the presiding officer's table at the front of the House chamber. Fite, while he was presiding, would sometimes invite a guest of honor to sit with him. On June 17, Brock was feeling pretty good about the way things were going as he sat next to Fite at the speaker's table. He had made a lot of progress in a few weeks in Montgomery. He was literally closer than anyone else to the power that ran at least half of the Alabama legislature, and he sat in a seat that told the world what he had accomplished. Then a reporter entered the chamber and approached Brock. What was Brock's reaction, he wanted to know, to Judge Thomas' just-announced decision that Central could not merge with State National. Grandeur suddenly came crashing down. "That was a bad day," Brock mutters, shaking his head.

No one ruled the Alabama Senate like Rankin Fite ruled the House, and Senate Banking was no "graveyard committee." Jimmy Clark, its chairman, was something of a banker himself. He made his living primarily in the real estate and insurance business, but he and a brother had organized the Citizens Bank of Eufaula in 1965. Clark was chairman of the $6-million bank, although a man named Harry Nelson was its chief executive. Clark was an apparent adversary to Brock on this issue. When 21 bankers met in April to organize the Committee to Preserve Local Banks, the small-town, anti-Central organization, Clark was one of them. It was he who introduced S245, the AlaBA bill, in the Senate on May 20. Moreover, as chairman of the banking committee, he had strong ties to AlaBA and the banking establishment.

Clark may have been the bill's sponsor, but he was in no great hurry to move it forward, perhaps because of the impasse in the House. Morris kept prodding for action but was hampered by the fact that AlaBA had two big causes to fight for in the 1969 session. Efforts to pass a new Uniform Consumer Credit Code, one that contained more accommodating interest rate limits for bankers, were meeting with strong opposition. That legislation endured an eventful summer, and Morris and his bankers often sought help from Clark with the consumer credit bills. It was a summer of trade-offs.

Clark finally scheduled hearings on the anti-branching bill for July 30. Those hearings became the focal point of the conflict, as both sides brought in their best arguments and their most able spokesmen. No formal record of that hearing was kept. The fullest (although unabashedly biased) account of what happened is contained in Morris' AlaBA "Bulletin":

> The hometown bankers, brilliantly led by Chairman of the Committee to Preserve Local Banks, Mary George Waite, presented a telling story to the Senate Banking Committee. Mary George began with sound and succinct arguments against statewide branch banking. She pointed out the value of the home-owned local bank to the hometown local businessman, farmer and housewife. As leader of the proponents, she then introduced the other witnesses. First on the list was H. O. "Hot" Glass of Thomasville. In a beautifully documented paper, he outlined the dangers of a concentration of economic power. . . .
>
> Next on the agenda was the hometown bank slide film. . . . It appeared to make a profound impression on the Banking Committee members. Speaking last for the hometown bankers was Past President Marshall Dugger of Tuscumbia. One of Alabama's finest orators, he told moving stories of his fifty years of experience in banking as he emphasized the value of the hometown bank to its own community.
>
> As expected, Harry Brock led the attack against the Hometown Bankers Bill. His arguments have been heard many times before, and no new elements appeared. Harry presented his case well here as he has always done before. Following his presentation, he introduced a businessman from Birmingham, who spoke in his behalf, and a farmer from Falkville, who is a customer of State National Bank and who spoke in favor of statewide branching. Bob Lowry of Huntsville appeared in opposition to both the merger and the Hometown Bank Bill.
>
> Following opponents of the bill, Representative Harry Pennington from Huntsville made the rebuttal for the proponents. He dissected the issues and stated the hometown bankers' answers to our opponents arguments specifically and incisively.
>
> Both sides of the issue presented forceful, hard-hitting testimony. It was, however, presented in gentlemanly terms, and

> personalities were kept out of the discussion. Some forty hometown bankers from all quarters of the State were on hand to listen to the proceedings and to offer support to those who were speaking for them. At the end of the hearing, as the crowd was dispersing, Committee Chairman Jimmy Clark made the comment, "That sure was a good hearing — well stated and not repetitive. The bankers always do things well."

Brock was feeling a bit beleaguered and plagued by rumors coming from Decatur. Only three days after the hearings, on August 2, he had to write to Nelson to try to hold back the anti-merger talk:

> A disturbing thing cropped up Tuesday night and Wednesday morning. Several Senators on the Committee said they had been told that Mr. Morris was saying that State National was cancelling the merger. I was asked if this was so, and I denied it. One Senator said that if this is going to happen then we should go ahead and pass the Bill because obviously the Board of Directors of State National doesn't care whether they merge or not. It put me in a very uncomfortable position!
>
> Now I hear that you are talking to Advisory Board members and others about the futility of continuing the merger agreement. You must know that when you do this it raises questions in the minds of many people, which in turn produces rumors and false information.
>
> I am aware that you would personally like to scuttle the merger, but please remember that you occupy a fiduciary position in this matter, and until the Board of Directors takes official action, I think that it is improper for you to drum up support among officers, stockholders, and others for the abandonment of the merger agreement.

A vote on the bill was scheduled for August 5. If the bill came to a vote in the Senate Banking Committee, nine members would decide its fate. Besides Clark, there was Hugh Morrow III, from whom Brock had wrested control of State National the summer before. There was Walter Givhan of Safford, chairman and majority shareholder of the $3.5-million Planters & Merchants Bank of Uniontown. There was Alton Turner of Luverne, who served as attorney to several small banks and who had been helping AlaBA notably with the mini-code. There was Jim Adams of Dothan, the hometown of one of Central's most relentless opponents, Wallace Malone; there was Pat Lindsey of Butler (and a director of the $5.7-million First National Bank there), who had introduced a bill prepared by Central that would allow statewide mergers. There was C. C. Torbert, Jr., of Opelika, whose father was president of the $9.5-million First National Bank there. There was W. E. Oden of Russellville, the chairman and president of the town's $5-million City National Bank, and there was Dan Stone of Centre. AlaBA was pressing for a vote, anxious to bring the bill before the Senate, where a decisive vote for passage could provide enough pressure to spring the bill for action in the House.

Alabama kept no records in 1969 of committee proceedings. There is no official record of a committee vote, and the press did not report a vote. But the committee did vote, Brock recalls well, and it occurred sometime between August 5, when we know a vote was scheduled, and August 28, when Morris reported defeat in a "Bulletin." Central stunned AlaBA by winning a squeaker, 5-4, according to Brock's recollection. Clark voted for the AlaBA bill, along with Adams, Stone and Torbert. Voting against were Lindsey, a Brock friend; Givhan, a friend of Ed Lowder's; Oden, a buddy of Fite; Morrow, and Turner, as Brock remembers it. The real surprise, Brock says, was Turner, supposedly a sure AlaBA backer. "Alton Turner cast the swing vote that defeated the bill," Brock recalls. That vote broke the bankers' back. After struggling all summer to get a vote, they finally got one and lost. Brock was exultant. "They must have thought they had the votes, because they were pushing for a vote. It turned out they didn't have them. Somebody didn't count right."

Getting a head count was not so simple, Morris counters. "You can never know until the votes are cast where politicians stand. They'll tell you one thing, then tell the other side something else."

Brock had evidently found the controls in both houses of the Alabama legislature and beaten the establishment bankers at their own game. There was one final flurry of activity in the House over the banking bill during the last days of the legislative session. Snell got the word that he should reintroduce his bill and did so. This time it was assigned, as he recalls, to the Judiciary Committee, chaired by Hugh Merrill of Anniston, the speaker pro-tem of the House. Brock, in a panicky moment, rushed to Fite, who told him not to worry. "I had been planning a fishing trip to Canada," Brock remembers explaining to Fite. "Go," Fite told him. Snell remembers some frantic last-minute parliamentary scurrying to try to short-circuit the normal procedures to get the bill to the floor before the session ended. He is uncertain if the Judiciary Committee ever voted on the bill, and the legislative record does not show even the bill's reassignment to Judiciary. At any rate, time ran out and the bill was lost.

The facts suggest that Governor Brewer, bowing to banker pressure in the last days of the session, intervened with Fite to get the bill assigned to a less moribund committee. Brewer does not recall intervening but says such a move was "quite possible" and consistent with how the governor did try to break legislative impasses. Brock is now certain that the bill was already sealed in its coffin before its reassignment. The last spasm of activity was little more than a tease. On September 4, the legislative machinery ground to a halt and the Capitol lapsed back into the tranquil domain of bureaucrats and office workers. By the time the lawmakers started up again, the horse was long gone from the barn and the opportunity had been forever lost to retain the "hometown" banking structure of Alabama.

"Harry Brock had little or no legislative experience at that time," explains Brewer, "but he came down to the Capitol and whipped all of them thoroughly. He took on one of the most effective lobbies in the state. They had the votes to pass the legislation, but Harry Brock used every parliamentary and procedural technique to win the fight. The bankers on the other side, particularly Wallace Malone, as I recall, were just adamant in their opposition — absolutely unyielding. This was really a crisis in their minds, and they took the loss as a devastating blow to banking in Alabama. Some of them were bitter at me for letting it happen. I had a frank, open relationship with Harry Brock. He came to see me and asked me not to get involved, said he thought he could win if the governor's office stayed neutral. That's all he asked of us."

Morris does not gladly reminisce about the 1969 session. "Like anything unpleasant, you'd rather forget about it," he points out. "I've never known an issue to be so intense. In my 25 years with the association, that was the most intense campaign," he says. "Brock was flamboyant and may have crystallized people's feelings, but it was the idea, not the man, that got all this going and caused so much intensity. Every legislative trick in the book was tried that session — either to pass the bill or to block it," Morris recalls.

Cook, the legislative veteran, has forgotten most of the details but remembers clearly the intensity: "Harry Brock got obsessed with it. The other side did, too. It was a nice fight, carried on on a high plane. But rough," he adds with a grin. "It was one son of a bitch."

Brock may have been fairly accurate in the early stages in depicting his opposition as coming out of the Birmingham board rooms, but as the campaign moved along, the small town bankers took on more and more of the fight against Central. By the legislative showdown, there was even a definite suspicion that the large banks were pulling their punches. Snell had plenty of votes lined up in favor of the bill, he recalls, but was noticeably short of votes from the Birmingham, Montgomery, Mobile and Huntsville delegations. "You couldn't help but surmise that the other banks were waiting in the wings, happy enough to sit back and let Brock work for them as the front man and take the flak and be characterized as a maverick and upstart," Torbert, now chief justice of the Alabama Supreme Court, recalls. "They had relationships with the small banks to maintain, and they kept the peace in AlaBA."

By all accounts there was little visible opposition to the anti-branching bill that wasn't coming from Brock and his Central-State National team. Lowry of Huntsville did testify against the bill. In retrospect, speculation centers on Frank Plummer, then president and chief executive of the First National Bank of Montgomery. "Once or twice I thought I might have detected the hand of Frank Plummer in certain events," Morris says. Curtis Springer, who represented Montgomery in the House, recalls a visit from Plummer in which the banker set forth his reasons for favoring multibank holding companies in Alabama and his opposition to the AlaBA bill. Springer agreed to oppose the bill. "Frank Plummer lived in Montgomery and knew many legislators," Bob Steiner, who was also First of Montgomery's attorney, explains. "I'm sure they knew his views on the subject, but we didn't launch a lobbying campaign." Plummer did more than simply sit on his hands, but his profile stayed so low that most observers marked him as "neutral." His own recollection is that he did not get involved in that battle, and Brock professes to be unaware of getting any assistance from Plummer.

The bankers seeking to preserve the old system of local community banks gave it their best shot in 1969 but lost. Hometown banks continue to prosper in Alabama and continue to act as a brake on the expansion of urban-based banking systems throughout the state. In 1987, Alabama still does not have full statewide branching. But a wave of structural change swept over Alabama banking in the wake of the 1969 legislative battle. The statewide banking Brock was seeking came to pass, although not quite in the form he had wished. Specific banks began to change hands with gathering momentum.

In 1972, Citizens Bank of Eufaula became one of the first banks to join Central Bancshares of the South, Brock's multibank holding company. Clark, who voted with AlaBA, became — and remains to this day — a Central employee.

Also in 1972, the First National Bank of Dothan became a founding partner of Alabama Financial Group. Malone, the archenemy of statewide banking, was named chief executive of the third largest bank holding company in Alabama in 1981.

In 1973, Rankin Fite, having been turned back by the state Supreme Court in his bid to claim cross-county branching rights, sold his bank to Alabama Financial Group, the forerunner of SouthTrust. He died in 1980.

Snell remains president of the Citizens National Bank of Shawmut, which is still a "hometown," independent bank.

CHAPTER SEVEN

Birth Of The Bancshares

BROCK WAS FUMING. It was bad enough that Frank Plummer had announced plans to form the first multibank holding company in Alabama, the basis for the first statewide banking system. To have come this far and then be beaten to the punch was downright frustrating, Brock found. And it didn't help matters any that Plummer's partners were Bob Lowry of First National Bank of Huntsville (a major competitor of State National and an outspoken opponent of the merger) and Jim Simpson and Norman Pless of the Exchange Security Bank. The hypocrisy of it all, he exploded. Plummer and First of Montgomery had been studiously neutral, but the other two banks had fought him every way they could, sometimes sanctimoniously, when he tried to move toward statewide banking. Now they were trying to do the same thing themselves while he was tied up in the Appeals Court, enjoined from merging because they were suing him.

Central and State National, after losing in Judge Thomas' Circuit Court, had activated Plan B and filed with the Federal Reserve System to organize a multibank holding company. However, the Fed had refused to act on the application while the lawsuit was still pending, Brock says. Central was stymied.

But what really made Brock's blood boil was that they had stolen his name. They were going to be First Alabama Bancshares. With typical foresight, Brock had considered that he might wind up forming a multibank holding company. If so, there was only one name for it: "First," because it would be the first one; "Alabama," because it would be a statewide organization. He had taken the precaution in 1969 of calling on Mabel Amos, the Alabama secretary of state, to reserve for his team the name First Alabama Bankshares, an understanding Mrs. Amos confirms. Brock reported the name to the Central board on August 11, 1969, according to the minutes. And now Brock learned in the summer of 1970 that Plummer, Simpson and Lowry were forming "First Alabama Bancshares."

Mrs. Amos now says that Brock lost the name due to a clerical mixup, the fault of a secretary in her office. But when Brock cornered her in July 1970, after he saw in the newspapers that Plummer was forming "First Alabama Bancshares," she told him that Simpson had come after the name — Senator Simpson, chairman of the State Personnel Board Simpson, her longtime friend and political colleague Simpson. What was she to do? She appealed to Brock, as he recalls. There was nothing he could do. Reserving a name with the secretary of state had no legal standing. There was no way to tie up legal rights to a name before forming the corporation. So Brock fumed and waited for the Appeals Court to rule on his appeal and waited for the Fed to rule on his application.

◇

Plummer had moved quickly once the legislature adjourned on September 4, 1969, without passing legislation to ban multibank holding companies. By September 23, newspaper stories appeared linking First of Montgomery, First of Huntsville and Exchange Security in plans to form a multibank holding company. Central, ironically, had made Plummer's job easier: "Brock advertising his State National deposits in Huntsville put the then president of First National Bank in Huntsville up the wall. We had no trouble getting him into the act," Plummer recalls. He declines to disclose reasons he had for thinking Exchange Security would also be receptive to joining the holding company, but Hurley recalls that Exchange Security officials, rightly or wrongly, thought someone might be attempting to buy up their stock in preparation for a takeover at about this time.

Plummer and Brock, the two pioneers of statewide banking in Alabama, are a study in contrasts. Plummer is as slight, frail-seeming and soft-spoken as Brock is gargantuan, robust and booming. Brock went candidly and energetically after what he wanted, bearing down in a direct frontal assault that eventually swept away or wore down his opposition. Plummer moved smoothly and quietly behind the scenes, planting suggestions, stroking egos, finessing his opposition into joining with him. It was New York and Hokes Bluff. The "silver fox" and the "big red roller," as they were sometimes called, steered clear of each other; neither tried to block the other or work together in any fashion prior to 1980. Yet they shared remarkably similar visions of where banking was headed and what Alabama needed to rise above financial provincialism.

Plummer had long believed that Alabama needed stronger, larger banks to stimulate her development. Multibank holding companies were the most likely vehicle for building a large statewide banking organization, Steiner had advised Plummer. Steiner, First of Montgomery's attorney, as well as a director and major shareholder, was a good friend of Plummer's, as was his father before him. Plummer had left First of Montgomery to become chief executive of Birmingham Trust National Bank, one of the state's two large, strong urban banks. He had made it bigger and stronger with the acquisition of the Bank for Savings. But he had alienated some of BTNB's powerful, ultraconservative directors and had left the bank just as its big merger was consummated. After some additional months in Birmingham, he returned to Montgomery to succeed Walter Kennedy as chief executive of First of Montgomery.

There was an element of exile in Plummer's return to the $200-million Montgomery bank, less than half the size of the post-merger BTNB. "We had no way to compete," Plummer recalls. "Four of our own directors were banking in Atlanta and getting the red-carpet treatment." He didn't like being too small to compete, and he had a score to settle in Birmingham and a rendezvous with history. His return to Montgomery in 1964 was linked to an agreement with that bank's board to investigate the formation of a multibank holding company. "I got the board, at our first meeting, to sign off that they had no objection to my forming a holding company," Plummer recalls.

He moved cautiously. One of the banks which caught Plummer's interest was State National, which by 1968 had outgrown the two large Mobile banks (Merchants and First

National) to become the third largest bank in the state. Plummer called him aside, Nelson recalls, after a meeting in Point Clear, to talk vaguely about linking the two banks. Plummer says he had considered trying to acquire State National, "but Brock beat me to the punch. I consider it quite a scoop." If round one went to Brock, round two was Plummer's. With the filing of his application to organize First Alabama Bancshares on July 3, 1970, Plummer was now out in front.

It was an exposed position, he found, and his effort now made him the target of attack by the opponents of statewide banking. A host of bankers from all over Alabama organized to oppose the application. They petitioned the Fed, which had to rule on the holding company application, to hold a formal hearing. In late September 1970, five stormy days of hearings were held at the Parliament House Hotel in Birmingham before Edward Creel, who actually worked for the Federal Trade Commission but had been drawn from a pool of hearing officers to come to Birmingham to conduct a hearing on behalf of the Fed. Wallace Malone of Dothan and Guy Caffee of BTNB were conspicuous in their opposition to the application. Small bank opposition also mobilized for the occasion, led this time by L. Y. "Yank" Dean of Eufaula. Brock attended the hearings and gave statements to the press during recesses. The multibank holding company, he predicted, would be good for Alabama.

Back in Washington, Creel recommended, on January 23, 1971, that the application be denied, and the Nixon Justice Department weighed in against the application on antitrust grounds. First Alabama appealed Creel's decision to the full Board of Governors. There, on April 21, 1971, the Board voted 5-2 to approve the application. On July 13, 1971, First Alabama Bancshares became Alabama's first multibank holding company and its second largest banking organization, surpassing BTNB in size. With $543.5 million in assets, it was second only to the $720-million First National of Birmingham. Plummer had fashioned a strong competitor and settled an old score.

It was becoming increasingly clear in the Central camp that their best hope was to combine Central and State National into the second multibank holding company in Alabama. On November 9, 1970, the Central board approved a resolution to form Central and State National Corp. of Alabama, a multibank holding company to be based in Birmingham. It authorized a 5-to-1 stock exchange for State National shareholders and called for a ten-man board, composed of the chairman, president and the three largest shareholders from each bank. On Friday, December 12, 1970, the application was filed. On April 7, 1971, the newspapers carried two items about Central. The bank had appealed its lawsuit to the U.S. Supreme Court, and the Fed had scheduled a hearing in Birmingham on the bank holding company application.

The Fed hearings were scheduled for May 13, a Thursday. This time the Fed sent its general counsel, Thomas O'Connell, as the hearing officer. In many ways, the one-day hearing was a compressed rerun of the First Alabama hearings. The same groups, using the same lawyers and the same arguments, opposed Central as had opposed First Alabama, although this time around First National of Birmingham took a more conspicuous leadership role, and BTNB and First of Dothan were quieter than usual.

First Alabama had set the precedent, but Brock was pulling out all the stops. When he learned a few weeks before the hearing that President Nixon would name him chairman of the National Alliance of Businessmen for the Birmingham area, Brock requested that the announcement be delayed until the afternoon of May 12. It was. When Brock showed up on the 13th, O'Connell called him over and congratulated him on his presidential appointment. O'Connell, a hard-driving attorney who brushed aside his diabetes and the blindness it was causing, memorizing relevant points of the banking law he could no longer read, recommended in favor of the application, and the Justice Department again weighed in against it. Central was still waiting for a verdict from the Fed on July 27, 1971, when the U.S. Supreme Court refused to hear Central's appeal, exhausting its legal avenues to a merger. It was to be a holding company or nothing. The vote finally came on October 8, 1971. The application squeaked by on a 4-3 vote in Central's favor. Central and State National were finally free to join together in a holding company.

However, the struggle was still not over. One more bitter battle remained to be fought before the union occurred, a battle to get State National shareholder approval. Rebellion still smoldered in the conquered kingdom, but this time the antagonists would be old allies, a falling out among the team that had staged the surprise coup back in the five frantic days of July 1968.

Throughout 1969, the Central crowd waged war in four different theaters. The first was the streets of Birmingham, where they continued to fight for new business and market share against strongly entrenched competitors. It was a battle they were winning. Central passed the $100-million mark in assets early in 1969, and closed the year at $113.4 million; earnings, at $986,936, fell just short of the $1-million mark.

The second theater was the federal court system, where Central fought its losing battle for the right to merge with State National, the goal behind the takeover. The third theater was the legislative halls of Montgomery, scene of the decisive victory over legislation that would have blocked Central from any form of expansion outside Jefferson County.

But the fourth theater was Decatur. The Central investor group had won a stunning victory in July 1968, but the legal challenges delayed the matter of "putting the two banks together" for three long years. Brock was the leader of an investor group that held 40 percent of the stock of State National Bank, but controlling a dominant block of stock was a far cry from controlling the bank. Neither Brock nor anyone else from Central was an officer or director of State National in 1968 and 1969. The bank was still largely controlled by its old crew. Their loyalty to Central, in some quarters, was tenuous at best, and Nelson had a solid majority of the board behind him in his effort to abandon the merger agreement. If Brock was to command State National, he needed to be able to do more than vote his stock once a year. He had to build a power base in Decatur from which he could direct State National during this indeterminable hiatus in his plans.

By the fall of 1969, while their merger was bogged down in the appeals process, while the State National board was paying only lip service to the merger agreement, and while Alabama was afire with rumors of holding company formations, Central moved to bring about some pre-merger coordination and cooperation between the two banks. At a joint meeting of the two boards in Birmingham on August 28, directors of both banks solidly backed filing a holding company application. By September 8, Brock could tell Central's directors that he had sold State National on increasing its board from 13 to 25 directors, a move approved by shareholders in January 1970. By October 1969, Brock was hired by State National Bank as a consultant. State National would buy two-fifths of his time and reimburse Central for two-fifths of his salary. In practice, it meant that Brock would work in the Decatur bank two days a week and spend three in Birmingham — if he weren't in Montgomery or in court somewhere. Besides being a consultant, Brock was named chairman of the Executive Officers Committee, a newly formed group that included Brock, Nelson, Hunter, Collins, Parker and F. A. Bloodworth. Although Nelson remained president of the bank, the powers of the chief executive were transferred to the Executive Officers Committee, where Brock increasingly had things his way. From the fall of 1969 until December 1971, Brock was the part-time CEO of two banks — 70 miles apart.

The proposal to stack the State National board ran into a legal challenge. Uncertain whether Judge Thomas' decision would survive the appeals process and sensing that Central could face serious obstacles because of the Williams Act violations, the Simpson lawyers Bobby Smith and Bill Somerville continued to press for a judgment against Central because of securities violations. When Brock sought to enlarge the State National board, Smith and Somerville asked Judge Thomas to enjoin him from doing so. Central rushed to file a report specified in Section 13(d) of the Williams Act just before a scheduled hearing before Judge Thomas. Both sides argued the merits of the Williams Act violations at a hearing in Selma on January 26, 1970. The judge denied the injunction, not because he concluded that Central had or had not violated the Williams Act but because he found that the plaintiffs would not be injured by allowing an enlarged board to sit. Legal sparring continued over the alleged violations of the Williams Act, but no judgment was ever rendered on this subject. The lethal bomb never exploded.

On January 27, twelve new members were elected to the State National board. The enlargement was cloaked in business development rationale: the new directors would help to bring significant new business to State National, which was no doubt true. But the list included Brock's great friend Red Leach, a Gadsden insurance man; Rex Rankin, a college buddy of Brock's and a Decatur insurance man; Carl Wittichen, a Central loyalist from Birmingham; Jimmy Hays, a Huntsville farmer, Farm Bureau executive and member of the investor group that seized control of State National, and Sam Pollock, Jr., a Gadsden automobile dealer and close associate of the Agricolas.

With an official management position, reporting directly to a friendly board, Brock set out in 1970 to start "realizing more of the potential" of State National. Most of Brock's changes were evolutionary and not controversial. They were also predictable, at least by anyone who had watched Central. Rankin was put in charge of a new Directors Business Development Committee charged with getting directors to bring more new business to the bank. Parker headed up an expanded marketing effort. Central and State National cooperatively formed a joint computer center.

In the face of what other directors began to call Nelson's "Brockitis," Brock worked to strengthen his support among the State National board. Conflict with Nelson came to a head in December 1970, and the board, at its December 8 regular meeting, had to intervene in "an apparent conflict among the executive officers." Nelson gave his account of the problem (not specified in the minutes), and then Julian Harris was called to explain the terms of Nelson's four-year contract with the bank. Nelson, Harris and all of the bank officers except Brock were then excused from a closed-door discussion which led to a resolution, passed 17-1, "that C. W. Nelson continue to serve as President of the Association, but that final decisions and operations of the bank be vested in the Executive Officers Committee as it is presently constituted and of which C. W. Nelson is a member."

The long delay in combining Central and State National was causing other kinds of problems for Brock and some members of his investor group. He was strapped. He was not a wealthy man, and he had not left Exchange Security to be a hired-gun manager. He was in the venture up to his eyebrows as an entrepreneur, an owner. Prior to July 1968, he was putting all he could save or borrow into Central Bank stock. He had exercised his stock option for 50,000 shares and bought additional Central stock. He owed Hamilton National roughly a quarter of a million dollars which he had used to buy Central stock and had secured with Central stock. When the State National takeover occurred, he went for a full participation, which meant he owed Bank of Virginia approximately three quarters of a million — for 7,525 shares of State National stock at the average acquisition price of $78.85 per share. He was a million dollars in debt.

Delays and uncertainty over the affiliation of Central and State National had helped to drive down stock prices. By August 1969, State National shares fell as low as $62; Brock was looking at a potential loss of $127,000 if he had to sell his stock. Fortunately, Brock notes, he had secured a two-year commitment from Rick Deane on the Bank of Virginia loan. "Being a prudent banker, he [Deane] might have felt obliged to call the loan when the price of the stock went down if he hadn't committed for two years. Then where would we have been?" Brock wonders.

To make matters infinitely worse, the late '60s and early '70s witnessed an unprecedented outbreak of inflation, leading to the Nixon wage-price freeze of 1971. Interest rates shot up to levels nobody had expected, certainly not Harry Brock. Both the Bank of Virginia and Hamilton loans were at 1 percent above the prime interest rate. Some of the investors had the resources to pay off Bank of Virginia and escaped a painful debt burden, but others saw their borrowing costs go through the roof as prime climbed from 6.5 percent in 1968 to 8.5 percent in 1969 and 1970. Brock was pinched as tightly as any of them. He squirmed in distress as he tried to keep up $100,000 annual interest payments on a salary and bonuses that grew from $57,000 in 1967 to $90,000 in 1970. He continued borrowing for things like school tuition for his children.

To make matters still worse, Central paid no dividends. By design and agreement with the regulators, all earnings would be plowed back into capital for the first few years. The no-dividend provision for Central had been written into the merger agreement with State National, and now delays were extending beyond initial expectations the time Central would return no cash to its investors. Brock feels certain that his adversaries were counting on this as they planned their strategy.

Brock and some of his Central investment partners had to have relief. On September 8, 1970, Brock presented to the State National board an amendment to the merger agreement, authorizing a special dividend to be paid by the two banks. A small flap ensued. Nelson proposed that State National pay a special 1970 dividend of $1.50 per share and that Central, reflecting the 5-to-1 stock ratio, pay one-fifth of that amount, or 30 cents. Brock, according to the minutes, argued that State National had paid a cash dividend of 75 cents for the second half of 1969 and would pay in 1970, with the special dividend, $3.00. Brock insisted that Central should be able to pay one-fifth of that amount, or 75 cents, effectively giving Central dividend rights, at the 5-to-1 ratio, retroactive to July 1969. Nelson balked at this, claiming that the 75 cents Brock wanted would violate the merger agreement.

A motion to defer a decision on the matter for one week was withdrawn without a vote, and counsel Norman Harris was summoned. Under the agreement, he told them, Central was entitled to only 30 cents unless stockholders of the two banks approved a different ratio. A motion to abandon the special dividend amendment apparently lost by a 9-to-8 vote, but the vote count was challenged. The motion was repeated and a roll call vote was taken. This time nine directors voted for the motion, nine against, with two abstentions. Chairman Wyker broke the tie by voting against the motion, so the proposal for a special dividend still faced the directors. Interestingly, Leach and Rankin were recorded as voting to withdraw Brock's proposal, while Agricola, Taylor and Nelson voted not to do so.

A compromise was put forward to permit Central to pay a 60-cent dividend. The compromise plan was substituted for the original amendment and then approved by the State National board, in both cases over Nelson's solitary opposition. A dividend to shareholders was in the works and was subsequently approved by two-thirds of both banks' shareholders at the December 1970 shareholders' meetings. At year-end 1970, Central paid its first dividend.

The dividend fracas was a warm-up to the real battle, which broke out over the 5-to-1 stock exchange ratio. That ratio had been set in 1968 by a New York investment banking firm, Keefe, Bruyette & Woods, in anticipation of a January 1969 merger of the two banks. It was accepted then without strong opposition from State National. Whether the same ratio would apply to the 1971 combination of the two banks in a multibank holding company became the last and, in some ways, the most bitter point of contention in bringing the two banks together.

Brock himself, in complimenting the State National officers at a June 9, 1970, State National board meeting, reviewed earnings for the first five months of the year and suggested, according to the minutes, that "Central Bank would have to work hard to maintain the 5-to-1 ratio in earnings." By October 21, 1970, State National's resistance to the 5-to-1 exchange had grown to the point that Central had to agree to a new review and Nelson could tell State National's directors that the New York investment banking firm of M. A. Shapiro Co. had been hired to reevaluate the exchange ratio.

Two things had happened in the two years from December 1968 to December 1970 that rekindled the stock exchange question. One was some relatively modest changes in the current financial statistics of the two banks going into the affiliation. The relative asset size of the two partners had shifted a bit as Central continued to outgrow State National. While Central would have provided 29 percent of the assets of the combined banks as of year-end 1968, that figure rose to 35.5 percent by year-end 1971. The book value of State National's stock continued to be more than six times Central's. On September 30, 1968, the numbers used to calculate the original merger plan showed Central with a book value of $6.27 per share, State National with a book value of $42.72 per share, a ratio of 6.8-to-1. By the end of 1970, Central's book value was

$8.75, State National's $55.43, a ratio of 6.3-to-1. The 5-to-1 exchange ratio would have meant a 27.5-percent premium over book value for Central shareholders in 1968, a 21.4-percent premium in 1970.

Earnings had shifted the other way. As Brock noted, State National was doing well. In 1968, 5-to-1 would have given State National shareholders a 3.2-percent premium in earnings. By 1970's net income figures, that exchange ratio favored Central shareholders with an 8-percent premium.

The other factor was a purely personal development that entered into no one's calculations but had effects strong enough to temporarily jeopardize the whole combination of Central and State National. Hugh and Joyce Agricola Parker were divorced. Parker had fallen in love with the widow of his wife's cousin and subsequently married her. Such a situation sent shock waves through a small town like Gadsden, and the rift left bitterness within the Agricola family. It was a civil divorce but hardly an amicable one, by Parker's account. He left Gadsden to take a rented apartment in Decatur, where he became an active officer in State National. Both Agricola and Parker continued to work closely with Brock in instituting changes at State National and preparing for a holding company. Brock often stayed with Parker at his apartment when he spent the night in Decatur, and the two men had long talks about the bank's future. As Parker recalls it, Brock indicated that they were partners and that he would run things in Birmingham while Parker ran them in Decatur, once the holding company was formed.

As a result of the divorce settlement, Parker's State National stock holdings increased, while his wife got more of the stock of Alabama City Bank, another bank in the Gadsden area in which the family had a major investment. By 1970, Parker was the largest State National stockholder, with 14,250 shares — more than Argicola's 11,000 shares, Taylor's 13,402 shares or the 9,232 shares held by the largest investor of the Brock group. He was also an ambitious senior officer of State National Bank, hoping to become its president soon. The years of waiting had undone the original agreement to make Nelson the chairman and CEO of the combined banks. He was only two or three years from retirement, and it was clear now that Brock would be chief executive of the holding company in name as well as fact, and that Brock would name the next president of State National once the holding company was organized. Nelson had become essentially a lame duck. Brock was in charge, with a trio of senior vice presidents filling out the Executive Officers Committee: Parker, Hunter and Collins. By Brock's account as well as Parker's, and according to the observations of more than one Decaturite, Parker had the inside track to the presidency.

But Parker was unhappy with the 5-to-1 exchange ratio. At the stormy December 8, 1970, meeting of the State National board, dissatisfaction with the exchange ratio boiled over. The Shapiro investment bankers had just issued a report recommending the 5-to-1 ratio. Nelson objected that this would mean an inappropriate premium to Central shareholders. An exchange of 5.75-to-1 would be more equitable, he said. Brock was prepared. He cited the Shapiro conclusion that "these exchange ratios (5-to-1) are fair and equitable to shareholders of both institutions." He produced a telegram from Hays, who was absent from the meeting, which advocated accepting the Shapiro report. Hays was part of Brock's investor group but owned much more State National stock than Central stock. Wittichen, the Central loyalist, rose to suggest that a deal was a deal and that both parties should stick to the 1968 accord. Leach, stating that he had roughly equivalent stakes in both banks, spoke in favor of 5-to-1.

Then Wyker recognized Parker. He strongly favored forming the holding company, Parker said, but the exchange ratio needed further study. Shapiro had used a different method to justify the 5-to-1 ratio than it had used in setting an exchange for First Alabama's formation. By applying the methods used by Keefe in 1968 but updating the data on which the Keefe decision was based, Parker came out with a ratio between 5.75- and 5.99-to-1. In 1968, State National would have sacrificed book value while Central would have sacrificed earnings under a 5-to-1 exchange; in 1970, State National would sacrifice both book value and earnings, he noted. While such a premium would be in order if State National were acquiring Central, it was not appropriate to two banks entering a joint venture, he argued. It was no academic question. The difference between 5-to-1 and 6-to-1 would mean $7 million to State National shareholders, he claimed.

Brock fought any delay. If the board approved the 5-to-1 exchange, the holding company application could be filed within a week, using June 30, 1970, figures. If approval were delayed until after year-end, the application would have to be refigured with December 31 statistics, causing a two-month delay in filing, he estimated.

But he didn't have the votes. Even Wyker and Taylor, who had been strong supporters of the holding company, favored 6-to-1. Leach withdrew his motion to approve 5-to-1, and the board agreed, by an 11-9 vote, to seek a joint meeting of both bank boards with Shapiro representatives.

At a special meeting in Birmingham one week later (December 15), after hearing from Shapiro representatives, Parker took the floor again, reviewing the Keefe and Shapiro reports and presenting his own analysis. The 5-to-1 exchange was unfair to State National shareholders, he insisted. A compromise motion was offered and passed, 17-3. It accepted 5-to-1, provided State National could declare a 10-percent stock dividend from its authorized, unissued common stock (the equivalent of a 5.5-to-1 ratio).

Wyker sought a private meeting with Daniel to see if the two chairmen could work out an agreement. Daniel was cordial, respectful and firm: it had to be 5-to-1. Wyker began to see little prospect of getting a better offer.

The State National board met again on December 18, three days after the 17-3 vote. Wyker bit the bullet. He asked for a show of hands of how many directors favored forming a multibank holding company. Every director raised his hand. Then he reported that Brock had told him the Central board considered the 5-to-1 ratio nonnegotiable. He moved acceptance of a holding company at a 5-to-1 stock exchange and was seconded by Taylor. A roll call vote then revealed that the 5-to-1 exchange had been sold; the board voted 17-7 to accept it. Opposed were Nelson and Richard C. Patrick, Jr., two of the old guard; Agricola and Parker, and three of Brock's additions to the enlarged board: Rankin, Pollock and Roy Drinkard.

According to Parker, Nelson had remarked during discussion that he disagreed with 5-to-1 but would go along with the majority. When the majority voted for 5-to-1, Brock asked Nelson to go along with the majority by changing his vote. Both Nelson and Drinkard did change their votes to give the holding company proposal a 19-5 majority. Pollock, who was on the other side, grudgingly gives Brock credit for forceful leadership. "I've never in my life seen anyone handle a group of 20 people like Harry Brock did. In those meetings he was in complete control at all times. He was smart and powerful, and he had smart, shrewd henchmen. They just railroaded that thing [the 5-to-1 exchange ratio] right through," he says.

Brock was still not out of the woods. To effect a tax-free pass-through of dividends from the banks to the holding company, the holding company had to own at least 80 percent of the stock of its member banks. Without 80 percent, earnings would be taxed at the bank level and again at the holding company level, effectively wiping out the holding company as a viable business arrangement. Parker was still fighting the holding company at 5-to-1, and Agricola, Pollock, Rankin and Patrick were lining up with him. The Agricola stock had made the State National deal for Brock in the first place. Now it began to look like it might unmake it. Parker alone held 4 percent of the stock. The five dissident directors together owned 9 percent. And they had ties with other shareholders. If they could convince holders of another 11-12 percent of State National stock not to exchange for holding company stock at 5-to-1, the whole plan would go down the drain.

Parker recalls this period as one of intense pressure. Brock used every means at his disposal to get Parker to give up his opposition, Parker recalls. Brock delayed picking a successor to Nelson until the exchange ratio was accepted. To Brock, Parker had stepped across a line and was no longer a principled advocate of an opposing position; he was a wrecker of The Cause. "He was trying to block the merger," Brock says in tones of moral enormity. In the end, Parker, the West Point man, did not flinch. He opposed the affiliation at 5-to-1 until the end and left the bank shortly after the final vote. The presidency went to Hunter.

The struggle left a bitter taste in the memories of all those involved. Brock calls it "the most unpleasant part of the whole struggle."

Since Parker would not cooperate, Brock had to find another way to be sure the holding company succeeded. One day in late 1971, not long before the stock exchange prospectus was to be mailed to shareholders, he and Red Leach paid a visit to Hugh Agricola in Gadsden. By the time the visit was over, Agricola had dropped his opposition, and Parker's cause was lost. It was a decisive visit. According to Brock, "We were just able to convince Mr. Agricola that a deal is a deal. We appealed to him as a businessman of integrity." Leach, the only other person still living who was present, says, "I think it was Harry Brock's ability to lay it all out in front of Mr. Agricola so that, being the businessman that he was, he could foresee what would happen from putting the two banks together."

Pollock, an intimate of both Parker and Agricola, insists that the divorce was pivotal to what transpired. "Hugh Agricola would have never gone with Harry Brock if it hadn't been for the divorce. He would have stayed with Hugh Parker, and there never would have been a Central Bancshares," he asserts. Agricola told his daughter and Parker that he had yielded to Brock's persistence. "They wore down his resistance," Joyce says. "He said he couldn't stand the pressure, that he was an old man and they wore him out, beat him down," Parker recalls.

With Agricola's support and Fed approval of the holding company application, success was assured. On November 7, 1971, the prospectus was mailed to shareholders, and by December 20, enough shares had been exchanged to make Central and State National Corporation official. The two banks were finally together, still two banks but one corporation, owned by one set of shareholders. A ferocious 41-month struggle was over at last.

CHAPTER EIGHT

The Rag-Tag Army

CENTRAL'S BOLD MOVE to take over State National set in motion changes that brought statewide banking to Alabama and the growth of large, sophisticated banking organizations beyond any the state had known up to that time. Like a brush fire, holding companies swept over Alabama in the early 1970s. First Alabama was the first, incorporated on July 13, 1971. Central was five months behind, on December 20. By September 1971, First of Birmingham had announced its intention to form a multibank holding company, and by October 6, it had found its initial partners: American National Bank & Trust Co. of Mobile and First National Bank of Decatur. Alabama Bancorporation, First of Birmingham's holding company, was formed on February 3, 1972, and became AmSouth in 1981. By October 20, 1971, BTNB and First of Dothan, the archenemies of statewide banking, had announced their intention to join Peoples National Bank of Huntsville in a holding company called Alabama Financial Group Inc. (later Southern Bancorporation, finally SouthTrust). That multibank holding company became operative on December 6, 1972. From their initial bases, these holding companies moved quickly throughout the state, acquiring other banks in major and minor markets.

One of the supreme ironies of Central Bank's history is that after daring so much and prevailing in its efforts to bring statewide banking to Alabama, Central was able to use the new expansion opportunities less than its change-resistant rivals. In the acquisition sweepstakes that followed the taking of State National, Central ran fourth among the four major banking organizations that emerged by 1973. State National may have been the crown jewel of the state, but there were other diamonds, and Brock spent the '70s watching them go to his competitors. "Our growth through acquisition has been by far the smallest of any of the big holding companies," he notes.

The name Central and State National Corp. lived only about a year. By January 23, 1973, it became Central Bancshares of the South, Inc. Central got a Montgomery affiliate, the $60-million Peoples Bank & Trust Co., under an agreement announced on February 21, 1972. Peoples had as two of its major shareholders Ed Lowder and Tine Davis. Lowder had helped Central get State National. Both Lowder and Davis, a Winn-Dixie supermarket executive, liked Central's style and wanted in. The three big shareholders — Lowder, Davis and Brock — made a fateful agreement: Central would not expand at the expense of present shareholders by paying dilutive premiums for acquisitions. They would strictly match book value to book value and earnings to earnings. On those terms, Peoples joined the system. The next bank in was Senator Jimmy Clark's $10-million Citizens Bank of Eufaula, under an agreement announced on May 1, 1972. Both Peoples of Montgomery and Citizens of Eufaula were formally acquired by the holding company on November 11, 1972.

On October 28, 1972, an agreement was announced to acquire the $18-million Deposit National Bank of Mobile County, headquartered in suburban Mobile (Prichard); it would give Central a presence in all four of the state's major metropolitan markets (Birmingham, Mobile, Montgomery, and Huntsville). A merger with the $21.6-million First National Bank of Auburn, where Lowder was also a major shareholder able to bring the bank to Central, was announced on November 14. On December 13, 1972, an agreement was reached with the $6.2-million Planters and Merchants Bank of Uniontown, Senator Givhan's bank.

In 1973, Central added the $20-million First State Bank of Oxford, a former "Hometown Bank" stalwart which was then seeking a partner and approached Central. In 1974, another troubled bank was added, the $3-million Sumiton Bank in Walker County. In 1978, Central acquired the $10-million Bank of Springville. Unwilling or unable to acquire banks in

Tuscaloosa or Dothan, Central started up new banks in those markets in 1975 and 1979, respectively. Then, on December 31, 1980, Central acquired from the FDIC the business of the failed East Gadsden Bank. In 1981, Central improved its position in south Alabama by acquiring the $79.6-million Baldwin County Bank east of Mobile and added to its size in Oxford by acquiring the $27.5-million First City National Bank there. These additions completed Central's bank acquisitions within Alabama to date.

By late 1981, when holding companies in Alabama had matured but not yet consolidated their member banks, Central had enlisted 12 banks under its banner, compared to 14 for Southern Bancorp. (now SouthTrust), 18 for Alabama Bancorp. (now AmSouth), and 20 for First Alabama. At that point, only 22.75 percent of Central's assets lay outside the two big banks whose merger started it all. By contrast, First Alabama had 36.4 percent of its assets in banks acquired after its original three partners had formed the holding company. SouthTrust had 28.4 percent of its assets in banks added after its holding company was formed, and AmSouth had 22.5 percent but added substantially to that figure in 1985 by acquiring the $1.1-billion FirstGulf Bancorp. of Mobile. All of the major holding companies but Central made post-1981 acquisitions. Central clearly did not add acquisition assets or new markets throughout the state as quickly as its major competitors did.

Looked at another way, the top 12 metropolitan areas of Alabama are Birmingham, Mobile, Montgomery, Huntsville, Tuscaloosa, Dothan, Gadsden, Decatur, Florence, Anniston, Phenix City and Selma. In Birmingham, the largest franchise went to AmSouth, the second to SouthTrust, the third to First Alabama, the fourth to Central. In Mobile, the two dominant banks were acquired by AmSouth and First Alabama. The third was earlier bought by AmSouth, and SouthTrust picked up the fourth. Central came in a distant fifth, although it added substantially to its market share in 1985 when it picked up eight offices (and $100 million in deposits) divested by AmSouth in its FirstGulf merger. In Montgomery, First Alabama took the largest; the second largest is still independent. The third largest went to AmSouth, and Central took the fourth. In Huntsville, the largest bank joined First Alabama. The second largest was acquired by AmSouth, although Central, through State National's Huntsville operation, came in a close third. In Tuscaloosa, the only substantial bank that joined a holding company went to First Alabama. Shut out, Central started a new bank there. In Dothan, SouthTrust got the biggest, with First Alabama second and AmSouth third. Central started from scratch in this market as well.

In Gadsden, AmSouth got the largest bank, but Central, thanks to Agricola's First National Bank of Gadsden, picked up a strong second place. Central was solidly first in Decatur, with second place going to AmSouth. In Florence, the largest bank remains independent, but State National's strong franchise there gave Central a solid second. In Anniston, SouthTrust, First Alabama and AmSouth finished one-two-three, and Central remains shut out. In Phenix City, the two largest banks remain independent, and First Alabama picked up the third largest. In Selma, the largest local bank is still independent. The other two major banks went to First Alabama and AmSouth, and SouthTrust picked up a small number four position. Central remains excluded.

Only in Decatur did Central get the largest franchise, only in Gadsden and Florence the second largest. Huntsville is the only other major market where Central could buy into the top three.

Other organizations, notably First Alabama, were able to bring in one strong, high-earning franchise after another, fueling growth and profits; Central assembled a rag-tag army of leftovers and good but tiny country banks. Central did not stop growing rapidly, but, having opened the door to statewide expansion through acquisitions, it used that door less than its rivals and turned, as we shall see, to other ways of "buying" assets and deposits.

There were two reasons for this weak follow-up to its spectacular acquisition, through State National, of a whole region of the state, the equivalent of several banks. The first was that many other banks in Alabama did not want to merge with Central. The merger season followed so closely on the heels of the legal and legislative battles that Central and Brock were still pariahs when the mating began, costing Central even serious consideration by several prime merger candidates.

Furthermore, Central was so aggressive and Brock such an intimidating CEO that the executives of other banks feared, with reason, that they would lose their power, decision-making authority and local autonomy if they affiliated with Central. They had seen what happened to Willard Nelson.

Multibank holding companies were successful in America as much for public relations reasons as for legal and financial ones. Bank affiliates in a holding company were still semi-autonomous banks with local boards of directors and a local president who retained prestige and varying amounts of executive responsibility and power. The holding company lessened the feeling that ownership and control of the bank had passed out of the community into the hands of outsiders. Alabama duplicated the experience of state after state. Holding companies were a necessary bridge to statewide branching, an indispensible sugar-coating to the consolidation process.

The key negotiator in most bank sales was the chief executive, the top professional manager. He wanted a good return for his shareholders, of course, but he also wanted to keep the perks and privileges of his position. A few CEOs happily negotiated themselves out of their jobs, but most preferred to affiliate with the organization that would give them the greatest autonomy. The holding company, essentially a decentralized form of corporate organization, met this need.

The multibank holding company was a shoe that Brock managed to get his size 12C foot into, but it was never a perfect fit for Brock or for Central. In a way, the decision to pursue a direct merger with State National instead of a holding company was a major strategic mistake. "Willard Nelson always wanted us to form a holding company, and he was right," Brock admits. "We would still have had opposition, but we could have been first and had a good head start on the others," he says. Central could probably have formed the state's first multibank holding company in 1969, without long delays and sizable legal fees and with less recrimination from other banks. A stronger organization might well have resulted. But the merger was truer to the corporate spirit of Central. It quickly became the most centralized of the holding companies, and the presidents of its affiliates became less important than line officers with systemwide responsibilities on the holding company level. Central's acquisitions, including State National, were quickly renamed as Central Banks, while other holding companies let affiliates keep their old names.

Bank stock analyst Jon Burke of the Robinson-Humphrey Co., who has followed Central for many years, observes that Central adopted a more centralized management because more of its affiliates had weak local management. That may be true; Central officers today consider some of their worst mistakes of the 1970s to have stemmed from allowing local banks to retain too much authority. But the converse is also true. Sensitive egos managing local banks knew they would have less real power if they joined Central than if they joined one of the other holding companies. It is no accident that most of the acquisitions Central did make were of fire-sale merchandise where local management was discredited or were banks delivered by major shareholders. Shareholders liked Central just fine, but it made professional managers nervous.

For once, the master of PR was done in by bad PR. The marketing whiz could not fashion the product the marketplace wanted: a low-key, reassuring club of semi-autonomous banks operating under an umbrella organization which left local banks largely undisturbed and treated local managers deferentially. Organizations which did market or at least advertise such arrangements made more sales.

Brock saw clearly what was happening. "Old Frank Plummer would put on his white hat and assure every president of every little old bank that he could continue to run his own show any way he liked, and that First Alabama never intended to merge all its banks, even if the law permitted it. And he signed up a lot of banks with that line, even though they will all be merged someday. We were up front with the banks we talked to and didn't make any secret of our intention to merge all our banks as soon as we were allowed," he explains.

The other major factor that reduced Central's growth through acquisition was the organization's pricing philosophy. The premium State National paid to acquire First National of

Gadsden back in 1964 made a lasting impression on Brock. That generosity made State National vulnerable to takeover, as he had proved. It was not a mistake he intended to repeat. Then, too, he was the largest single stockholder of Central Bank and the leader of a tight-knit band of original investors. It went against his grain to reward stockholders of newly acquired banks at the expense of old stockholders. So Central, which had always been more willing than its competitors to pay the price for growth in the Birmingham market, found itself priced out of the merger market.

No-premium stock-exchange mergers flourished as "mergers of equals" in the 1980s, but in the early 1970s, the price for acquiring a good bank was often a substantial premium. The biggest one that got away, the one that hurt most, Brock recalls, was the City National Bank of Tuscaloosa, the onetime Morrow bank that nearly beat Central to State National. "We could have done City National in Tuscaloosa for 5-percent dilution," Brock recalls. "They wanted to come with us and would have done so for 1.14 percent of book, but instead they went with First Alabama for a 1.35-percent premium. That's the best bank First Alabama bought," he says with obvious regret.

"It was our strategy to grow market share, without many mergers and without taking dilution," Brock explains. "If I had it to do over, I would try my damnedest to do more mergers and take early dilution. We had an economy in the 1970s with a lot of growth and high inflation that overcame most dilution quickly. The other banks turned out to be right to pay those premiums for their acquisitions." He is no longer bound by the old no-dilution agreement he had with Lowder and Davis, he notes.

So Central, the invincible, infallible darling of the 1960s, the bank that apparently could do no wrong, had a mixed record in the early '70s. It had made mistakes, but it still closed out 1975 as a $1.07-billion bank holding company, the fourth largest banking organization in the state. Any student of bank holding company expansion would have confidently predicted in 1968, given Central's size, growth and market position, that it would be an early acquisition by one of the major banks in

Montgomery or Mobile (or possibly Decatur) that wanted a good Birmingham foothold. Instead, Central beat long odds to become an acquirer and the flagship of one of the four banking giants of Alabama.

CHAPTER NINE
Growing Pains

WHEN THE STATE NATIONAL takeover uncorked three and a half years of turmoil, Central was a four-year-old, $82-million bank. It was tightly wound and running all out. Growth had been heady, and it was solidly in the black, but it was still a little bank. Management depth was suspect, to say the least. Top management was Harry Brock, who was personally energizing and directing almost all of Central's activities and single-handedly making nearly all of the executive decisions. No other staff member was — or had ever been — more than a vice president.

The staff was good and highly motivated but dependent on Brock. Central operated like a little bank — full of teamwork without much organization. Bookkeeping for all of the bank's accounts was still being done manually. Even before the takeover occurred, the bank was experiencing growing pains, feeling a strain to keep the organization in step with the rapid growth of its business.

The takeover and its spreading consequences diverted a great deal of Brock's attention from Birmingham banking. It created substantial legal, lobbying and public relations expense. The controversy caused uneasiness among the bank's corporate customers, particularly its correspondent banks. Like all mergers, it created concern about individual careers. Moreover, economic difficulties loomed just over the horizon. The Lyndon Johnson guns-and-butter economy was sending high inflation Central's way, and 1974 ushered in the worst recession in the bank's brief history.

The period of July 1968 through December 1971, while the external battle raged, posed a serious internal challenge to the fledgling organization. Ambition had unleashed a swarm of besetting difficulties. To continue to flourish, perhaps even to survive, Central would need more resources than it apparently had. The newcomer was off for a test drive down the north side of Red Mountain.

Central could hardly pass through the experience unscratched, but it emerged in remarkably good shape. The bank closed out 1968 in style.

Financial Performance 1968-70

	1968	1969	1970
Assets	$98 million	$113.4 million	$137.4 million
% change	+24%	+15.5%	+21%
Deposits	$85 million	$98.2 million	$120.6 million
% change	+26%	+15.4%	+23%
Loans	$47.8 million	$58.7 million	$62.8 million
% change	+69%	+22.8%	+7%
Net Earnings	$873,681	$986,936	$1.5 million
% change	+39%	+13%	+48.2%
Return on Assets	1.01%	0.93%	1.17%
Return on Equity	17.3%	20.2%	28.4%
Capital/Assets	8.1%	6.6%	6.3%
Chargeoffs/Loans	0.066%	0.13%	0.25%

Deposits were still cheap, with demand deposits making up nearly 75 percent of deposits, CDs only about 14 percent. About $1 million was added to capital, largely from internal sources. The tilting of the bond portfolio toward tax-exempts, begun in 1966, continued. Perhaps the only cloud lay in a 53-percent increase in operating expenses. Interest on deposits was still a very modest 27 percent of operating expenses, but personnel expenses now topped $1 million annually, and other expenses, perhaps reflecting some merger costs, exceeded $900,000. The new headquarters and new branches had practically doubled rent from 1967 levels, and the capital notes issued in 1967 had created an additional interest expense. Central was outgrowing its low-overhead beginnings.

In 1969, growth tapered off radically. The bank's funding mix did not change drastically, but inflation-fueled interest rates caused a 92-percent increase in interest paid for deposits, and interest-bearing deposits increased 25.5 percent. Interest on deposits, for the first time in Central's history, catapulted into the largest operating expense category. Personnel expenses continued to rise; the 28-percent gain for 1969 was more than twice the 13-percent gain in net income. Other expenses increased a bit less than 12 percent in a year when legal and lobbying expenses would have been heavy. Capital additions of slightly less than $1 million were all generated internally.

Central was back to a banner year in 1970. Aside from a 29-percent jump in personnel costs, expenses generally stayed flat. Interest on deposits even declined a bit. Checking accounts continued to comprise more than 70 percent of deposits, while CDs had gradually increased to 18 percent of deposits. Spreads were still good. Deposits which had cost the bank $1.6 million funded loans and securities which earned $6.8 million in Central's last year of bachelor reporting. Beginning with 1971, consolidated earnings would be reported, reflecting the combination of Central and State National, then other members of Central Bancshares.

Capital was boosted by just over $1 million in 1970. Earnings were nearly $1.5 million, but Central's first dividend, paid in 1970, distributed almost half a million dollars to its patient investors.

Such was the story of the publicly reported numbers. The bank was obviously avoiding serious trouble, continuing to grow and make a reasonable profit, despite the special expenses and considerable distractions. Behind the scenes, the same general impression prevailed, but there were unmistakable sounds of heavy breathing as the bank labored to modernize and automate its operations, rein in expenses, improve staff and refuel the fires of enthusiastic salesmanship. In August 1969, the bank hired its first professional personnel director, charged with developing a staff training program. Management was structured in 1969, as three men were raised to senior vice president and put in charge of divisions: Rains over lending, Tate over marketing and Everett A. Phillips over operations. Floyd Jones, the bank's original cashier and charter member of the "Spirit of '64," became one of the casualties, people who did not want to keep pace with the bank's rapid growth. Jones signed on with the organizers of a new bank in Five Points West, and Brock reported to the board on February 10, 1969, that Jones "left with our best wishes and that we had solicited the correspondent account and offered to help them in any way possible."

The alliance with State National came at an opportune time for Central's fraying operations. State National had a computer system and had automated its accounts. Central had not, but by February 1969 the process of using State National's computer to automate Central's accounts was underway. Brock told the board that savings accounts would be on the computer by March, loans by April and checking accounts by no later than July. So 1969 became a conversion year, and Central's monthly business reports were disrupted by unavailable information as accounts were in the process of being computerized. Going onto the computer, Brock told the board, would help decrease expenses.

Examiners arrived in July 1969, and complained of having to spend too much time reconciling accounts in bookkeeping, proof and the general ledger, but the problem was ascribed to the computer changeover, according to the minutes.

In July, Phillips delivered a detailed report on monthly income and operating expenses for June. He concluded:

> Advertising, conversion, merger and a few extra employees to train to replace those leaving contributed to wrecking the budget for June in the amount of $51,012.77. With positive effort we can approximate budget by year end. Enough corrective action should be taken by the end of August to get us back in line. We are over for the year $64,320.87.
>
> Total Income continues over budget $9,283.34 for June and $384,873.31 year to date. Unless our deposits increase substantially, we can't expect much more income from loans and investments than we are presently realizing.
>
> Hopefully, we will not have to borrow funds in July as we did in June. This cost us about $16 thousand net income after taxes for the month of June as compared to May. Having to sell Government Bonds during June to meet cash cost us income as well as sales. The income loss cost us about $10,000 of net after taxes income.

While the report frets over lost income and budget-wrecking expenses, it is worth noting that it reports expenses that are $64,000 over budget for the year to date and income that is $384,000 over budget. It is also worth noting that July's long meeting, with all of its attention to computer conversion, capital increases, problem loans, additional branches, more business, examiners' reports and expense control occurred at the height of the legislative battle in Montgomery, while the appeal of Judge Thomas' verdict was being prepared and while Brock was arm wrestling with State National directors over their support of the appeal and even the merger itself. The minutes of the July 1969 board meeting paint a convincing portrait of a bank, during one of the most turbulent months of its hectic existence, that is being elaborately and meticulously managed.

Brock was able to bring some good news to that meeting. A report showed that of 966 banks organized in the U.S. since 1963, Central was the third largest as of December 31, 1968, when its assets had reached $94 million. Only 24 of the banks were larger than $34 million in deposits. Given Central's rapid growth in the first half of 1969, Brock suggested, there was a good chance Central had raised its standing to second or even first place. Its growth was good not only by Alabama standards: Central was a national phenomenon.

The pattern of responding to incipient problems with careful measurement and concerned management continued throughout a difficult year. In September, the board minutes record that "Mr. Brock reviewed, in detail, an analysis prepared by the Business Development Department on our progress year-to-date. Our projected growth for the year 1969 was set at $24 million. To date we have attained $17,738,081.67. Washing out the temporary deposits of approximately $8 million in the Daniel accounts, this leaves us way behind our projection for the year. The Business Development analysis goes into detail concerning the results of the directors, officers and employees."

Later in that same meeting, "Mr. Brock reported that our expenses exceeded our *pro forma* by $53,196.96 for the month of August. Our income exceeded our *pro forma* by $23,967.75. We are hopeful of still obtaining our goal of earnings of $1.50 per share. However, this goal will be most difficult to make if our deposits are not substantially increased between now and year-end. According to calculations we are on the projected amount of $1.30-per-share earnings at this point."

This meeting occurred while Central was investigating a multibank holding company and while Brock was getting the State National board enlarged and getting himself added to State National's management.

In 1969, Central also undertook a survey to determine the bank's image in the Birmingham community at the suggestion of Harry Bandouveris, the political PR man who had created the football cartoons and was now Central's advertising director. The survey of 2,096 opinion leaders (the same group to whom Central was mailing propaganda about its proposed merger with State National) confirmed that the bank was making a favorable impression. It ranked first in its market as the fastest growing, the best looking, the most modern and the most aggressive. It also drew top scores for having the best ads, the lowest loan rates, the highest deposit rates and the most accommodating loan policies.

Other qualities showed room for improvement. Despite its Saturday hours, Central was picked by only 8.7 percent of the respondents as most convenient. It was not considered as successful or as secure as its large rivals, and it came in fourth (in a field of five) for friendliness, although the scores were all close together. It scored particularly low in bank officer depth, and it came in a distant third for providing the best service and for doing the most for the community.

The survey also revealed that Brock was more widely recognized as CEO of his bank than were any of the other local bank presidents and that 12 percent of those questioned identified George Wallace with Central Bank.

The bank moved quickly to shore up its image for civic-mindedness. It became a patron and adviser to the Birmingham Ballet, and Bandouveris developed a series of public service advertisements that drew comment. One supported American forces fighting in Vietnam. Another, linked to a local arts festival, saluted Great Britain with a tribute to Sir

Winston Churchill and prompted an appreciative note from Churchill's widow.

Central, through 1969, watched with interest as the New York prime interest rate rose. In February, the board acted to link Central's pricing formula to the New York prime, setting its best rate at half a percentage point below the New York prime, which was 7 percent at the time. In June, when the New York prime hit 8.5 percent, Central decided to freeze its own prime at 7.5 percent for established borrowers who kept deposits in the bank. A memorandum from Brock informed commercial borrowers of Central's decision to price below the New York banks and "the two largest banks in Alabama." The decision not to raise rates, he concluded, "is our way of saying thank you for doing business with us."

Correspondent banking, despite the ideological clash with small banks over statewide banking, continued to grow. A report offered at the November board meeting showed that balances had risen to $18.5 million for October 1969. Balances, starting at $200,000 in September 1964 when the first correspondent customers were signed up, had increased quite steadily, averaging $3.5 million in 1965, $7.8 million in 1966, $10.2 million in 1967, $13.9 million in 1968 and $16.3 million over the first three quarters of 1969.

Capital was a nagging problem. While retained earnings kept feeding the capital accounts, capital growth could not keep pace with balance sheet growth and capital ratios had fallen below regulatory thresholds. Central had to raise new capital, but the merger agreement with State National and the complications and delays in organizing the holding company greatly limited Central's options for raising capital in the marketplace, so capital offerings were discussed and delayed. By 1973, with capital scraping at 5.5 percent of assets and Central Bancshares stock thriving in a general boom for bank stocks, it was time to raise capital. Central prepared a $15-million offering four months after Central's first stock split, effected in the form of a two-for-one dividend.

Timing the offering was important. It was an obvious advantage for Central to get the best possible price for its shares. So Brock followed an Alabama connection to Wall

Street, where he sought out Jon Rotenstreich, the son of an old friend and one of the youngest managing partners at the prestigious investment banking house of Salomon Brothers. Under Rotenstreich's direction, the stock offering was readied, then delayed several times as market complications arose. "It was like a space launch," Carolyn Robertson recalls. Finally, on April 19, 1973, the stock was offered. It brought $26 a share, hitting almost perfectly the crest of the appetite for regional bank stocks. It sold at 21 times earnings and four times book value, Brock notes, and occurred just before a ten-year price decline. "Two weeks later — maybe even two days later — we couldn't have done it," Brock observes.

When only half of the $15 million was picked up by common stock investors, Central placed the other $7.5 million in subordinated convertible notes with Morgan Guaranty Bank & Trust in New York at 5.5 percent interest. The 47-percent increase in capital in 1973 brought the capital back up above 7 percent of assets. The stock offering, Central's last to date, was largely ignored by the original investors, who were enjoying the appreciation of their $2, $5 and $10 shares but may have considered $26 a high price to pay for the stock. (At $26 a share, Bill Daniel's risky initial investment of $10,000 was worth $260,000, and Brock's $100,000 stock option incentive was now worth $2.6 million.) Outsiders bought most of the 1973 stock, raising the number of Central shareholders to over 5,000. "It was a Wall Street deal, not an Alabama deal," Brock notes. Central placed two other notes, for $10 million and $5 million in 1977 and 1978 respectively, but otherwise has relied on earnings to build capital.

Business development campaigns, so crucial to Central's success, were subject to continual renewals. Human beings, Brock knew from Dale Carnegie and his own experience, were leaky vessels where inspiration and motivation were concerned. Leave them alone, and they would go flat. They had to be pumped up fairly often, and the record makes it clear that Central's sellers were not left unpumped during the crush of lawsuits, lobbying and arm-twisting. In July 1968, just days before the takeover of State National began, Burroughs *Clearinghouse,* a complimentary banking magazine with a large national circulation, hit the streets with a feature article on Central's successful use of directors to bring in business. Brock had thousands of copies reprinted and spread them around to show everyone the favorable report. Central had revitalized its director solicitation program at the start of the year. Each director pledged to work one full day every month to bring business to the bank. Directors Tom Jernigan and John Evins, two of the board's top salesmen, were named co-chairmen of the business development committee. The full board would meet monthly at 7:30 a.m. for special sessions dealing exclusively with business development. A goal of $92 million in deposits by the end of 1968 was set. Competition, prizes and an endless sequence of progress reports continued unabated.

The business development program needed pumping up again by January 1970. This time the job went to Tate. The bank had missed its 1968 goal of reaching $92 million in deposits by some $4.9 million. In 1969, Tate explained to the board at its January 1970 meeting, 12,000 new accounts had been opened with opening balances of $44 million but the bank had experienced a net deposit increase of only $13.2 million. The 1970 goal was $20 million in new deposits. The $20-million goal was broken down into $4 million to be brought in by the directors, $3 million by the advisory board, $2 million through an employee incentive program, $1 million from pre-approved overdrafts on checking accounts, $5 million from new public funds and $5 million from growth of correspondent bank balances.

To make sure the bank got its $20-million deposit gain, Tate reported that Central would also seek $1 million from customer referrals from correspondent banks, $1 million of new business from national accounts, $1 million raised through new branches and a half-million from a "Save for College" program. He cautioned that opening balances would have to exceed $20 million considerably if Central was to reach the goal of a $20-million deposit increase.

The report continued, according to the board minutes:

> Local Business Development Calls will have to be considerably improved and new people have already been added to the Business Development staff for this purpose. Mr. Tate stated

> that the Directors had been assigned an Officer of the bank to work with them on local calls, and at this point Mr. Brock emphasized that it would be the responsibility of the Officer to motivate the Board member and at all times have available a backlog of prospects to call upon.

The burden for business development was clearly shifting to the staff. By July the bank had a formal "Staff Sales Training Section." Tate's program evidently worked, because deposits for 1970 increased by $22.4 million.

Operations problems continued to nag the bank. Director Marshall Durbin pointed out in the January 1970 meeting that "help is needed in internal operations and auditing." Computerization had not eliminated earlier problems. By September 13, 1971, board minutes record Durbin as complaining that "there were evident problems concerning the flow of work from the tellers to proof to computer. He stated that he was aware that part of these problems was the use of inexperienced personnel and supervisors and that it is evident that we need more capable, better-trained personnel. He said this again emphasized the necessity of keeping our training programs in effect and looking ahead so that we will be geared up to handle our future growth."

Correspondent banking balances continued to grow. At the May 11, 1970, board meeting, Tate reported that Central had picked up 21 new accounts in Tennessee since the beginning of the year, bringing to 174 the total number of banks using Central as a correspondent. By December 1971, Tate was able to tell the board that Central, with correspondent balances of $42.8 million, ranked first in Alabama in correspondent balances.

◇

In the fall of 1971, while Central was waiting for the Fed to rule on its application to form a bank holding company, there occurred one of those bold, inspired public relations coups that punctuate Central's history. The Alabama legislature, following a political stalemate, adjourned without passing an appropriations bill for the fiscal year beginning October 1, leaving the state legally broke and unable to meet its payroll.

Brock was in Washington when he heard about the state's financial crisis. He found a phone and called Taylor Hardin, the Alabama finance director. "What are you going to do?" Brock wanted to know. According to Brock, Hardin told him, "You're the banker. You tell me what we should do." Brock promised to think about it and come up with something, Hardin recalls.

It wasn't long before Brock called Hardin back — this time from the Atlanta airport — with a proposal. The two men worked out a plan, then put it to work. State employees were paid on schedule October 1 with warrants from Central Bank, essentially interest-free loans advanced by Central to state employees, repayable when the legislature approved funding for the state. The state treasurer printed the warrants, using payroll records, but Central put up the funds, or at least a substantial part of the initial funds, to meet the first $3.65-million payday. The *Wall Street Journal* and Alabama newspapers played up the story, frequently quoting Brock. When pay for teachers was in jeopardy, Brock publicly offered to pay them too, with interest-free loans, if local banks did not come forward. It was, Hardin reflects, "risky, even foolhardy at first, but then the other banks began to get jealous of the attention and felt left out. They petitioned to get a piece of the action."

Other banks did share in the funding. According to the *Wall Street Journal,* Central, First of Birmingham and First of Mobile all shared in meeting the first payroll, but it was Central's idea and Central's first commitment; Central got most of the credit for rescuing the state in its hour of need.

Four paydays came and went during the funding emergency, with no employee suffering any disruption in income. Wallace joked that the system worked so well he didn't need to fuss with the legislature to get an appropriations bill. Brock asked for more state deposits to help Central offset its costs of meeting the state's payroll, but the treasurer balked and sought other banks to put up additional funds. Finally, during a special session of the legislature called by Governor Wallace, an appropriations bill did pass, and the state repaid the banks. The situation returned to normal. Central lost some income on the funds it advanced but reaped a large harvest of favorable publicity for civic-mindedness and for leading the other banks in the state. The *Wall Street Journal* certainly was received and read at the Fed. There is no evidence that the favorable national publicity that appeared only days before Central's application was approved, 4-3, had anything to do with the decision, but it would hardly have hurt.

The whole payroll crisis episode gave rise to a story that Brock insists is true. He had found time to go dove hunting during this period and had shot more than his limit. A game warden came along and demanded to see his license. "Brock?" the warden pondered. "That name sounds familiar." "It should," Brock retorted, "It's on your paycheck." As the warden moved away, a dove reportedly rose from some nearby bushes. "Yonder goes one. Get him," the appreciative warden is supposed to have shouted.

◇

Operations were still ragged in 1973, when Central threw the problem to M. Douglas Mims, an early Central employee who had been running the branching system. According to Mims, "The bank had such tremendous growth in the first eight years that the ox was in the ditch before we noticed the problem. We had no operations professional to start with. Our expertise was in loans." Mims left Central in 1974, somewhat dissatisfied with what was happening, and shortly thereafter became the superintendent of banks for Alabama.

Frustration with continuing operations problems probably contributed to his decision to resign, but Mims was also unhappy with other strains brought on by the bank's rapid growth. He talks vaguely about flowering egos, short tempers, petty complaints, ingratitude, intemperate criticism and misplaced credit for the bank's accomplishments. It was not, from Mims' perspective, as happy and harmonious an organization in 1974 as it had been in 1964. "From day one until the State National takeover, morale was just great. Every employee felt totally responsible to the bank. I don't think we ever lost a competent employee from when the bank opened until a year or two after the combination with State National," he recalls. There were some sharp growing pains in the early 1970s.

One of the sources of pain within the organization, by several accounts, was Clyde Tate. Tate's influence had soared and he was, by 1972, arguably the number two man in the company. The original executive officers of the holding company were Brock as president, Tate as vice president, Parker as secretary-treasurer, and John Hendrix, Brock's all-purpose staff man, as assistant secretary-treasurer. Tate ranked with Rains, Phillips and Mims as senior vice presidents of Central Bank in 1972, but more than a few insiders considered him first among equals after Brock. He had built the hugely successful correspondent banking department, and his marketing division was responsible for business development, sales training and advertising, all favorite activities at Central. Moreover, only Tate among the top officers shared with Brock a bold, entrepreneurial imagination and an appetite for one-on-one salesmanship. "They were two of the best salesmen and best idea men you'll ever find," Rains says of Brock and Tate. No one could match them when it came to brainstorming. Central got its reputation as a daring bank on the strength of their ideas, and the ideas that were actually used paled by comparison to the wild inventiveness of some of the ideas that were discarded as too bizarre or too risky, associates report.

Tate is described by close associates as a driven and hard-driving man, an intense person, fast talking and fast moving, who could be irritable and impatient with his subordinates but also paternal and compassionate. He relished competition, idolized athletic leaders like Alabama football coach Bear Bryant, and threw himself into business contests like a charged-up linebacker. He was afraid, Rains recalls, that he would die young and was determined to live intensely while he could. He was emotionally volatile.

Rains and Mims give remarkably similar accounts of Tate's role at Central in the early '70s. Tate was a natural resource, valuable to Central if properly managed and directed. Only Brock could control Tate, and as Brock was pulled away from the bank to be in Montgomery, Decatur, or Washington, Tate began to cause friction within the bank.

By 1973, Tate was considered a problem. Some thought he was burning out. He had accumulated too much baggage from past battles, others suggested. There was a perception, says Rains, that Tate's effectiveness was somehow wearing out.

Matters came to a head in January 1975. Tate left the bank, and shortly thereafter bitterly made it known that he intended to form a rival bank. There were Central officers who were committed to Tate and would follow him, everyone knew. Brock called the staff together and asked his officers to choose right away whom they would follow. Jim Lovell, who had been with Central since 1966, left soon thereafter. Others followed over the next ten months: William R. Weatherly, like Lovell a vice president in the correspondent department; Loxcil Tuck, one of the early Central fanatics; Gerald Touger, Central's auditor; then-State Representative Jabbo Waggoner, Central's director of governmental affairs; and Joe S. Brown, once the bank's personnel director. It appeared to be a substantial loss.

The new bank, Southern National, would be another fast-starting Central, the defectors told each other. Sometimes there was even a suggestion that Central was becoming staid and bureaucratic and that it was time for a new maverick to come along and stir up the waters and try bold new approaches. It was to be a wholesale bank, Tate decreed, with a strong correspondent department. He had the satisfaction of opening the bank on September 12, 1975, and claiming to have the largest first-day assets of any bank ever to open in Alabama. Two months later, on November 11, 1975, he died from a massive heart attack at the age of 46. Southern National was closed by the regulators on June 14, 1979, a casualty of bad loans.

CHAPTER TEN

The Mature Bank At Work

CENTRAL BECAME A BIG BANK during the '70s. It kept much of its hustle and continued to ask for the business. It remained politically active and courted publicity. It continued to grow rapidly if somewhat erratically. And it was still Brock's bank, a daring entrepreneurial venture, quick to try new things, seldom moderate when it could be radical, an anomaly among Alabama banks, although its wildest adventures were behind it once the holding company was formed. In many ways it remained remarkably true to its origins and founding philosophy. But it changed fundamentally the ways it went about its business and made money during the 1970s, partly as the hand of Terry Brannon was increasingly felt in its management.

Brannon was Central's enduring whiz kid. He joined the bank in 1968 as an assistant vice president in real estate and started the '70s as vice president for real estate credit. By the end of the '70s he was president and chief operating officer of the holding company and Central's number two executive. He was not as convivial a personality as Brock but was one of Central's most cerebral bankers. Brannon knew the numbers inside and out, and he was not afraid to disagree with Brock. He was a resourceful entrepreneur in his own right and provided some of the sophistication and management depth that Central needed to succeed as a big bank.

The young Central had a clear formula for generating profits: grab all the deposits you can get, especially the free ones; make safe loans and put the rest in securities; keep expenses low except for salaries and advertising, and show the customer you appreciate his business.

The Central of the '60s was deposit-driven. Rapid growth came from the bank's formidable skill at gathering funds. It was hard to find enough good loans to get loan-to-deposit ratios much above 50 percent. During the '70s, Central switched to being an asset-driven bank. Growth came to depend on the availability of attractive earning assets, which could always be funded in some way. Central's deposit-driven growth had been phenomenal. "We were adding $1 million a month in the beginning, then $1.5 million, then $2 million," Brock points out about the early years with obvious satisfaction. However, Central's growth through merger, after the huge acquisition of State National, was modest and generally finished by 1974. Central could have continued to grow by $1 or $2 million a month by hustling for local deposit dollars to lend or invest.

This was too slow, Central's leaders decided. The bank opted instead for a wholesale or money-center strategy. Lending would be aggressively pursued when economic conditions were favorable. Loans would sometimes be acquired wholesale. Central acquired a lot of automobile loans, for example, by buying them in quantities from auto dealers. Large deposits were essentially bought, increasingly in national markets, through competitive bidding. And so it was that Central came to add $219 million in assets in 1972 (for an average of $18.2 million a month). And $188 million in 1973 ($15.7 million per month). And $265 million in 1976 ($22 million a month). And $282 million ($23.5 million a month) in 1977.

The investment portfolio — used conventionally by most banks to offset peaks and valleys in loan demand — came to be viewed at Central during the '70s as a profit-maker in its own right. If economic conditions created good loan demand and good investment opportunities, Central would expand in both, according to Brannon, and "buy" the deposits or sometimes nondeposit liabilities to fund the assets.

The funding shift is apparent in Central's activity in the Fed funds and repo markets, money markets used to quickly rectify shortages or excesses of liabilities and assets. A bank with excess cash will "sell" it to a bank that needs more money (liabilities) to fund assets — at a competitive market rate of interest. Central's use of these markets is colored by its role as a major correspondent bank. It would sometimes buy or sell to accommodate correspondents, not always to manage its own position. But the big shift from being a net seller to being a net buyer reflects the money-center strategy. In 1970, Central and State National combined sold $10.8 million in Fed funds and bought $3.15 million, to be a net seller of $7.65 million. By 1980, Central bought $209.7 million in Fed funds and repurchase agreements and sold $36.3 million, to be a net buyer of $173.4 million. Central had gone from lending its excess deposits to other banks to borrowing heavily from others to fund its asset growth. While total deposits grew at a 12.5-percent five-year compound growth rate from 1975 to 1980, Fed funds and repo borrowings increased by 41.2 percent annually, taking up the slack as asset growth exceeded deposit growth.

Central came to rely increasingly on certificates of deposit that could be acquired quickly through competitive bidding. From the beginning of the decade, there were no legal rate ceilings on what were called "jumbo CDs," those of $100,000 or larger. Smaller deposits were capped under Regulation Q, but banks were free to pay what they thought large deposits were worth to them. Organizations with more than $100,000 to deposit were likely to be sophisticated and rate sensitive. Purchased money flowed quickly to the highest rates. It was expensive money and potentially volatile money. It could leave in a hurry if a bank stopped paying top rates.

During the 1970s, inflation blew away traditional interest rate controls. Piece by piece, bank deposits were deregulated: interest rate controls were removed and deposit rates allowed to rise to competitive market levels. Central favored deregulation, which was rapidly narrowing the gap between purchased money and core deposits. It offered top dollar for 6-month, $10,000 CDs when this product was approved in 1978, then did the same thing for two-and-a-half-year "Small Savers" CDs in 1980 and for the $2,500 money-market accounts in 1982. While its rivals bought deposits by acquiring other banks, Central bought much of its rapid deposit growth in the marketplace by paying high rates.

The impact of this wholesale strategy on Central's cost of

funds was dramatic. In 1970, Central and State National together had 59 percent of their deposits in checking accounts, which earned no interest. By 1980, only about 30 percent of deposits were in checking accounts. Central and State National had to spend only 27 percent of income on interest expenses in 1970. In 1980, interest expenses ate up almost 61 percent of operating income.

It was clearly a strategy of going for higher volume at lower profit margins. Assets and liabilities would rise quickly in a successful wholesale bank. Earnings would also rise, but less quickly. By going wholesale, the bank would increase its profits — make more money through increased volume — but at a lower rate of profitability.

Central could expect to pay for its money-center strategy with a reduced return on assets. High-priced deposits held down the bank's return on assets (ROA) and equity (ROE) but less so than might have been anticipated. Central Bank and Trust (through 1970) and Central Bancshares (after 1970) recorded the following ROAs and ROEs:

ROA				ROE			
1964	1.15%	**1976**	1.00%	**1964**	10.6%	**1976**	15.24%
1965	1.04%	**1977**	1.31%	**1965**	21.9%	**1977**	20.8%
1966	1.46%	**1978**	1.10%	**1966**	33.7%	**1978**	17.3%
1967	0.96%	**1979**	1.06%	**1967**	17.6%	**1979**	15.1%
1968	1.01%	**1980**	0.90%	**1968**	17.3%	**1980**	13.2%
1969	0.93%	**1981**	0.50%	**1969**	20.2%	**1981**	8.6%
1970	1.17%	**1982**	0.91%	**1970**	28.4%	**1982**	14.2%
1971	1.20%	**1983**	0.93%	**1971**	20.4%	**1983**	15.0%
1972	1.00%	**1984**	0.90%	**1972**	25.7%	**1984**	14.0%
1973	0.97%	**1985**	0.98%	**1973**	23.9%	**1985**	15.3%
1974	1.07%	**1986**	1.05%	**1974**	22.6%	**1986**	16.4%
1975	0.76%			**1975**	10.0%		

Obviously something bad happened in 1975 and something even worse in 1981, which call for explanation, but except for those years and unusually high earnings in 1966 and

1977, Central fairly consistently hovered around the ROA high-performance benchmark of 1 percent under both its old deposit-driven strategy and its new asset-driven strategy. Its combination of internal growth and high earnings were enviable by national standards. Color graphics in the 1978 and 1979 annual reports show Central, for the years 1972-79, running anywhere from 2 percent to 5.85 percent ahead of its peers in the Southeast in return on equity and between 0.17 percent and 0.32 percent ahead in return on assets, according to norms published by the Robinson-Humphrey Co.

How did Central maintain such generally good returns while the price it paid for its raw material, money to lend or invest, went up so drastically? First, it went after high-yielding assets. The 1980 net interest margin of 5 percent was the lowest in Central's history up to that time, but it was still a financially healthy margin. Second, the bank gave up less of its net interest income to overhead. A wholesale operation could run cheaper than a retail one. It could spend less on brick and mortar, and loans bought in bulk from automobile dealers did not require salaried lenders. Noninterest expense grew by only 11.9 percent a year, on average, from 1975 to 1980, while noninterest income grew by 14.9 percent. Although Central is not a big fee-income bank, trust fees, service charges on accounts and other sources of fee-income offset only 16 percent of the bank's operating expenses in 1970 but grew to 30 percent by 1980.

Two other factors had a major impact on the bank's bottom line: profit taking from the securities portfolio and tax refunds. While many banks held onto high-yielding securities for their future earnings value, Central traded aggressively and was not averse to selling securities at a profit. Securities profits or losses were negligible through 1976 but added more than $3 million to after-tax profits in 1977, more than $1 million in 1978 and nearly $2 million in 1980 (after a loss of $613,000 in 1979).

Even more important to Central's profits was a tax strategy adopted by the bank in the mid '70s. Congress laid the groundwork for the strategy in 1975, when it tightened one tax shelter (the amount of earnings that could be socked in the loan loss reserve) but liberalized another: the length of time a bank could recover previously paid taxes during tax-loss years. Central had a bad year in 1975. Its earnings (before taxes and securities transactions) were $6.9 million, the least money the bank had made since the 1960s. This qualified the bank for a tax refund of $1.2 million and started Brannon thinking. Central, like virtually all other profitable banks, had been paying taxes — typically $2 or $3 million a year. In early 1976, that money, in Brannon's mind, formed a $11.5-million pool Central could get back and add to its income if it could show losses to the IRS.

All banks keep at least two sets of books, one for shareholder accounting, another for IRS accounting. The rules are far from the same. It was not unusual for a bank to make money and pay a dividend to shareholders while showing a loss to the IRS and qualifying for a refund of previously paid taxes. But it was unusual to mold a bank's business plan around a tax strategy to the extent that Central did.

It was no fun to get refunds by actually losing money, Brannon knew. For the plan to work, the bank would have to maximize its tax write-offs while realizing a lot of tax-free income. Here the special conventions of banking prior to the Tax Reform Act of 1986 came to his aid. Banks routinely invested in tax-exempt securities, primarily bonds of state and local governments. The interest earned from such investments was not taxable, but a bank could borrow money to buy the securities and, before 1987, fully deduct from taxable income its interest expense. The income from the assets was tax-exempt, while the cost of the assets was tax-deductible. Brannon went to the accountants with his idea. They thought it would work. Then he went to Brock, who liked it.

Central had favored tax-free bonds for a number of years as a way to reduce its tax burden. In 1972, state and municipal bonds made up 70 percent of a $174-million investment portfolio. But in 1976, the portfolio ballooned to $500 million. U.S. government agency bonds were virtually liquidated (falling from $18.6 million in 1975 to $5 million in 1977). Tax-frees, meanwhile, jumped from $115 million in 1974 to $346 million in 1976 (still 70 percent, but 70 percent of a much larger portfolio). Maturities in the investment portfolio lengthened substantially as the bank added longer term tax-frees to maximize yield. By year-end 1977, 71 percent of the tax-frees matured in five years or longer; 51 percent of the total investment portfolio carried maturities of five years or longer. Some 25 percent of assets were in tax-free investments.

The tax harvest was spectacular. In 1976, pre-tax earnings recovered somewhat, rising from 1975's $6.9 million to $7.9 million, while the tax refund jumped from $1.2 million in 1975 to $3.8 million in 1976. It was even wilder in 1977, when pre-tax earnings jumped smartly to $11.3 million and the tax refund still increased to $3.9 million. In 1977, Central's bottom line, its profit after taxes and securities transactions, was $18.5 million, compared to income before taxes and securities transactions of $11.3 million. It had turned the normal situation upside down. Taxes were earnings: after-tax income exceeded pre-tax income. The bank earned nearly as much in 1977 from taxes and securities transactions ($7.2 million) as it had earned from operations in 1976 ($7.9 million).

Another $2 million in taxes flowed back into the bank in 1978. Central briefly reverted to a more normal experience in 1979, paying a modest $608,000 in taxes and taking a $613,000 loss in securities transactions, as the tax pool receded. The bank returned to form in 1980 with a $2.4-million tax benefit and a $2-million securities gain as it finished cashing out its previously paid taxes.

Central's money-center strategy was successful in that it let the bank expand rapidly while reducing overhead ratios and maintaining attractive earnings. Central avoided one of the risks inherent in the strategy: it did not deflate its earnings through a rapid increase in its cost of funds. It was able to compensate by finding high-yielding assets and increasing noninterest income. But two other time bombs were ticking. They would rock the banking industry nationally, and they would bring great pain to Central locally.

The first one exploded in 1974 and 1975. It was a serious economic recession, the worst in many ways since the 1930s. It had a devastating effect on banks in the South. C&S of Atlanta, the bank Brock used as his model in building Central, lost

$17.8 million in 1975, then another $10 million in 1976. In the first quarter of 1977, it suspended its dividend at the insistence of regulators and did not resume it until the third quarter of 1978. On February 27, 1978, Richard Kattel, its president and the successor to Mills B. Lane, was forced to resign. Things were even worse in Chattanooga, where Hamilton National Bank, Central's original sponsor and principal correspondent for many years, was closed on February 16, 1976, at that time the largest bank ever to fail in the South. Many banks saw earnings plunge precipitously if they did not entirely disappear. Things were somewhat better in Alabama, although the state's economy was still quite vulnerable to recession.

The recession attacked asset quality. Many loans that were safe in a good economy quickly fell to past-due status in the bad recession. Banks that had most aggressively expanded assets (like C&S and Hamilton) were most vulnerable. Central had taken on great asset risk with its expansion. Loan losses had been negligible, far below those of most banks, through 1972's $563,000 (0.13 percent of loans). In 1973 and 1974, losses rose noticeably, to 0.37 and 0.36 percent of loans, respectively, still quite good by industry standards. In 1975, they hit 0.94 percent of loans, better than C&S's worst year (1.9 percent in 1977), but two and a half times more than Central had ever charged off in a year before. Asset opportunities dried up quickly in 1974, and Central's growth ground to a virtual halt: 4.1 percent in assets, 5 percent in deposits, 1.2 percent in loans. Only $35.8 million in assets were added in 1974, by far the smallest percentage gain in Central's history, all at a time when normal growth easily would have put the company over the $1-billion mark in assets. The $1-billion landmark would have to wait until 1975.

Central's recession experience was bad but brief. Earnings plunged about 19 percent in 1975, reflecting the large chargeoffs of that year, but the bank was back on a growth track before 1975 ended and recorded a 15.5 percent asset gain for the year. Loans had been charged off aggressively. Lower chargeoffs and strong collections of loans previously charged off dropped net chargeoffs to 0.70 percent of loans in 1976, then to 0.50 percent in 1977 and 0.40 percent in 1978. Earnings rebounded to a record $11.5 million in 1976. The tax strategy took effect by 1976, and Central was off to an absolute banner year in 1977. By 1978, the bank was clearly taking in sail and bracing for adversity again. Due to the momentum of 1977, earnings were still good, but asset growth slowed to 1.7 percent.

Particularly significant was an $89-million contraction in the bond portfolio and evidence of the bank's flight from tax-exempt bonds. " . . . The sale of a substantial portion of our tax-exempt bond holdings early in 1978 brought our taxable income above tax-free income during the last two months of the year," Brock explained in the annual report. The second time bomb was ticking audibly now, and Central had heard it. The 1978 annual report was full of talk about asset/liability management and Central's determination to "decrease the need to purchase expensive rate sensitive funds, and more closely match the mixes of assets and liabilities as to rates and maturities."

The money-center strategy had produced a liability structure that was both expensive and volatile. If interest rates went up or down dramatically, liabilities would reprice relatively quickly. If assets were slower to reprice, the bank could get clobbered in a rising-rate environment. Central was now a liability-sensitive bank and distinctly vulnerable to a rate rise. Thanks to formula pricing and a history of prime-based lending, many of the bank's loans were market-linked and would reprice quickly. Others, like the car loans, were fixed-rate assets, however. Particularly dangerous was the bond portfolio crammed full of five-year, ten-year and even 15-year tax-free bonds. Central had earned an enviable tax-equivalent yield on its tax-frees in 1976, 1977 and 1978, but if rates rose substantially, those bonds could quickly change from buoyant life preservers to lead weights.

If rates rose by half a percentage point as they normally did, it wouldn't be catastrophic, but inflation was making the markets turbulent. If there was another record jump of 3 percent, as there had been in 1974, the bank would surely suffer. Fixed-rate assets were being evacuated as quickly as possible to alleviate the damage, but it was a slow process. By year-end 1980, only 47 percent of loans were rate-sensitive. Investments were in worse shape. In 1979, Central took its first taste of bitter medicine: $613,000 in securities losses to purge some low-yielding government bonds, which brought net earnings slightly below 1978 levels. The flight from tax-exempts continued: from $346 million in 1978 to $288 million in 1979, back up to $317 million in 1980, down to $292 million in 1981, $272 million in 1982, $241 million in 1983 and $238 million in 1984, while taxable securities were rising from $110 million in 1978 (less than one third the amount of tax-exempts) to $925 million in 1983 (four times the amount of tax-exempts).

Central couldn't move fast enough. In the fall of 1979, interest rates broke from an 11.75-percent plateau and climbed to 15.75 percent. Then in the spring of 1980, they shot up to 20 percent, the highest prime rate ever in the U.S. Rates plummeted during the summer of 1980, (down briefly to 11.25 percent) but soared again and closed the year at 21.75 percent. The roller coaster ride was on, and Central was turning green.

Prime stayed above 17 percent for nearly all of 1981, above 20 percent for much of the year. The bank's cost of interest-bearing deposits rose to 12.87 percent, more than double the rate of 1977, while asset yields grew more modestly to 14.74 percent. The spread between rates paid on deposits and earned on assets fell from 3.52 percent in 1977 to a skinny 1.87 percent in 1981. The worst spread problems came from the bond portfolio where the huge tax-exempt holdings were the boulder in Central's balloon. While Central's most rate-sensitive assets repriced from 5.97 percent in 1977 to 16.77 percent in 1981, the tax-free securities went from 10.62 percent to 10.66 percent (tax equivalent) during the same period. In attempting to throw overboard some of the dead weight, the bank took securities losses in 1981 of $4.5 million. Net earnings, typically $4 to $6 million per quarter, fell to $1.7 million in the third quarter of 1981, then to $1.4 million in the fourth. Net earnings for the year fell 62 percent from 1980's undistinguished level. Return on assets fell to 0.5 percent, return on equity to 8.6 percent. The bank met its $0.80 dividend, but it took 74 percent of the earnings to do it. "The last six months of 1981 were a disaster," Brock said in a 1982 interview. To make matters still worse, thin spreads and high chargeoffs ($9.1 million) ran the bank out of the taxable income, and the 10.66-percent tax-equivalent yield effectively shrank to the nominal yield of closer to 6 percent.

It was the worst business reverse the young bank had ever experienced. Central was used to winning; for the first time its executives saw up close the specter of defeat. It had been somber in 1975, but all banks were struggling then, Central less so than many. Now Central was suffering the consequences of its own strategies and sinking at a time when many of its peers and rivals were thriving. There was little actual panic. The bank still made more than $7 million profit. But there was plenty of anxiety, according to Brannon. Brock talked ominously about moving to "Phase Two" if the bank didn't get turned around soon. "Harry would never tell us what Phase Two was," Brannon reflects. "Phase One was our plan to get out of the pit. All we knew about Phase Two was that it was much worse." Phase Two turned out to be unnecessary. Earnings jumped from $7 million in 1981 to $23 million in 1982. Return on assets was back up to 0.91 percent, return on equity to 14.24 percent. Central was back on track, and its executives were smiling again. The spread between rates earned and rates paid fattened to 2.44 percent (from 1981's 1.87 percent) as interest rates receded to 12-16 percent levels and deposits repriced downwards faster than assets did.

"In retrospect, we didn't have as bad a year in 1981 as it seemed at the time," Brannon now concludes. "Then, some of us wondered if it was the end of the world."

Central countered the adversity with a characteristic show of strength: Brock sent each of the bank's 425 officers out into the streets for a massive business development campaign, first in Birmingham, then in Central markets across the state. The target was every licensed business in those markets — an estimated 75,000 calls. The best defense, he figured, was a good offense.

◇

Four years earlier, the end of the world stared Brock vividly in the face in a very different experience of vulnerability, one that disrupted briefly but tragically the essence of Central's business drive. None of the growth and strategic repositioning of Central caused Brock to move away from the key ingredient of his original formula for success. Using directors to bring new business to the bank remained a cardinal part of Central's strategy, but after the acquisition of banks throughout Alabama in 1972 and 1973, the job of motivating directors became more difficult. There were far more directors to pump up, and they were more dispersed. Most of them were inherited with banks that had not expected directors to actively solicit business. They didn't have the religion. It was time, Brock decided in 1977, to pump up the directors as a selling team and spread the religion around the statewide system. Each of Central's 12 banks had its own official board of directors, in addition to the Central Bancshares board. So it happened that Brock in the best Central tradition made a fateful decision. He would personally visit each of the system's 255 directors in the director's own place of business during 1977 to let each director know how important he was to the organization's success. It was a little bit crazy to spend that much of the chairman's time running around to Jasper, Dothan, Auburn, Oxford and Eufaula, but Central was a little bit crazy that way.

It was to be Auburn on Thursday, September 27. Central did not have a corporate airplane, but director Tom Jernigan did, and the bank had worked out an arrangement with Jernigan to use the plane sometimes — and Jernigan's pilot, 51-year-old Chester Collins, a small, wiry, grizzled veteran who was fond of telling people that there were two kinds of pilots: old pilots and bold pilots, but no old, bold pilots. The weather looked doubtful for the 27th, Collins told Brock the day before. Fog was distinctly possible. If Auburn fogged in, the trip would be rearranged, and they would fly to Montgomery and go on by car to Auburn. But Collins arrived late and out of sorts at the Birmingham airport that morning. They were flying to Auburn, he snapped to Brock and co-pilot Mike Parker as they took off at 6:45 a.m.

Auburn was shrouded in fog. The airport was not equipped for an instrument landing, but Collins radioed ahead and was allegedly told by the Auburn controller that he was 1.5 miles from the airfield, a communication the controller later denied. A faulty altimeter indicated that the plane was well above the ground when it began clipping through pine branches. They were in the trees. A solid pine bent the starboard prop and punctured the fuel tank as Collins fought for elevation, then simply for control of the plane. They continued in the air briefly and then jolted to the ground amid debris of torn branches. Brock and Parker were shaken up but not seriously injured. Collins was conscious but wedged in his seat by the dislocated controls of the plane. The plane was on fire and all of its doors were wedged shut by the shattered pines. Brock and Parker managed to force open a rear door and escape. Brock ran to a nearby house, first for a garden hose that was too short, then for an ax. He worked frantically to break the front windows to rescue Collins, but flames were spreading rapidly, sending smoke billowing through the cabin. Collins looked at Brock and shook his head and Parker yelled for Brock to get back before the plane exploded. Moments after Brock backed away, the plane exploded in flames, killing Collins quickly.

The incident spread shock waves through the bank, although the first word of the tragedy came when Brock telephoned, so his colleagues knew from the first that he had survived. For Brock, however, there was no escaping the nightmares that followed and lasted for years. It was a grim and rare experience of helplessness, but one which did not change the basic way Central went about its business. The corporation still does not have an airplane, however, and according to some insiders, it never will.

Brock's efforts did bear fruit, for 1977 became the best year ever for new business brought in by Central directors: $107 million, or $420,000 per director — well over the goal of $45 million. It once again brought media attention to the bank's prowess in salesmanship.

◇

Central emerged from the Valley of the Shadow of Financial Defeat in 1982, having barely escaped the rigors of Phase Two, in what looked at first glance like middle-class respectability. Gone from the annual reports were the prominent graphics demonstrating how Central consistently outperformed its Robinson-Humphrey peer group from 1972 to 1979 (its superiority to the average ROA and ROE achieved by banks with assets between $1 and $2 billion). In fact, after nearly bringing up the rear in 1981, Central was running with the pack in 1982, 1983 and 1984. Its earnings were surprisingly good in light of its narrower-than-average spreads, but its profit levels and its growth rate had become . . . ordinary.

The numbers are accurate and revealing up to a point, but Central remained a maverick and a hotbed of entrepreneurial banking activity. One flash of brilliance became apparent in 1982 with a most unlikely product: home mortgage loans. Central did not make mortgage loans. It was an article of faith, an unassailable assumption. Mortgages were the longest of fixed-rate loans, so Central stayed away from mortgages.

But in its pursuit of assets whose yields would rise and fall with interest rates, Central had pioneered the use of adjustable-rate consumer loans. The bank had introduced adjustable-rate auto loans to Alabama in 1981, and was doing a good business with three-year car loans with rates that could be adjusted every six months. People in the consumer lending area began to talk about extending the terms of adjustable-rate loans, even to 15-year mortgage loans.

The mortgage market at that time was bogged down under the heavy weight of high long-term rates engendered by the high inflation of the late 1970s. Variable or adjustable-rate mortgages were being actively discussed and introduced in some markets, but in Alabama in mid-1982, the only mortgage available was a 30-year fixed-rate mortgage at approximately 15 percent. Not surprisingly, high mortgage rates had caused a national housing slump and a growing reservoir of would-be home-buyers waiting for rates to come back down to affordable levels.

Conversation escalated to calculation in the consumer lending area and led to a startling discovery. The going rate was 15 percent. Central, if it did not have to build in protection against general interest-rate increases, could afford to lend at 12 percent. And if the lower rate were combined with the faster amortization schedule of a 15-year mortgage, a home buyer could actually make a lower monthly payment for a Central loan and pay off the loan in half the time! A $50,000 mortgage at 15 percent amortized over 30 years resulted in a monthly payment of $632.22, according to their calculations, while an adjustable-rate loan at 12 percent, amortized over 15 years, required only $600.08 monthly, assuming the rate stayed at 12 percent. So Jim Prince, a vice president in consumer lending, took the idea to the credit committee. They liked it. With rates that adjusted every six months, it provided a perfect asset to balance with deposits coming from six-month CDs.

Central had no mortgage lending department, but it did have a finely tuned sense of marketing and recognized the attractiveness of the product. If Central could beat the other banks to the punch with an affordable mortgage product, it would have a window of opportunity through which it could feast alone on the pent-up demand for housing. So it struck quickly and boldly, using full-page newspaper ads to trumpet the advantages of the product. The window stayed open for an entire year, and the bank which started without a single mortgage loan on its books ended up with half of its consumer loans and nearly 20 percent of its total loan portfolio in adjustable-rate home mortgage loans, all in a little over two years. It was a characteristic Central success: a good idea, a good feel for the market, and quick, decisive action to scoop its more cautious, slower-moving rivals.

Another stellar performance, less meteoric in its rise but equally brilliant in its result, was taking place in the investment banking division, where years of what Brannon calls "grinding it out" were paying off, making Central the dominant investment banking bank in Alabama and the third largest in the Southeast (behind Union Planters and First Tennesse, both of Memphis).

Again the key was salesmanship. The bank embarked on a strategy, starting in the mid 1970s, of using its investment department not primarily to manage the bank's own portfolio but to aggressively sell securities services (mostly bonds) to large corporate investors and a few wealthy individuals. The profits came not from correctly predicting the course of the markets but from the steadier stream of commissions earned on transactions. It was a low-risk, low-margin, high-volume business; at least the volume became high by 1986, when Central sold $54 billion worth of bonds to garner gross trading profits of almost $26 million. Those revenues compared to $13 million in 1985, $6.75 million in 1983, $2.95 million in 1980 and $233,000 in 1977.

Central's $13 million of trading profits in 1985 stacked up against $7 million for NCNB, $6 million for Wachovia, $4 million for SouthTrust and $3 million for AmSouth (but $71 million for Union Planters and $26 million for First Tennessee). When the combination of thin commissions, aggressive selling and top-flight, well-paid investment pros (led in the mid '80s by Bob Neumeier) clicked, Central pushed the strategy for all it was worth, expanding into the Midwest and opening its first out-of-state investment office in Louisville in 1986. If the company's bottom line (which *was* getting pretty flashy again in 1986) seemed ordinary for most of the earlier '80s, it was not because Central was getting fat and complacent. Lines higher up in the financial statement revealed Central to be a bonanza player, innovating, taking chances, pressing for the big strike.

Brock began to goad his organization to sharpen the quality of its services in the early 1980s. Suppose the bank, he once asked a group of senior executives, promised publicly to pay customers $10 for every mistake it made in handling the customer's account? The executives blanched and stammered and the $10 was never offered publicly, but Brock's point was made. Dan Puckett, responsible for the branching system, hired outside "shoppers" to visit every branch, unknown to the branch staff, and measure everything from waiting time in teller lines and the cross selling of bank products to the maintenance of the parking lot. Back-room controls were also implemented.

Brock was also pushing for a revival of the sell-like-hell spirit. New competition, much of it from hard-selling organizations like Sears, Merrill Lynch and Prudential Insurance, was making even traditional banks try incentive programs and talk about paying its customer contact people by commission.

Central was already a leader in the use of incentive programs, but the industry was not swinging toward a "sales culture," and Brock did not intend to be outsold. Central would have to make a radical shift from paying people by salary plus incentives to paying people by straight commission. Attention focused first on the visible personnel in the branches: tellers and new accounts reps. A pilot program, begun in 1984, was endorsed and expanded so that by year-end 1986 all of the new account people were paid completely on commission. The transformation was traumatic. "We had a lot of turnover, and we expected that," conceded Puckett, "but we are emerging with a happier, more productive, better-paid sales staff in our branches." For employees who hung on and made the transition, the change meant increased uncertainty and anxiety but also bigger paychecks, according to Puckett. Those who two years earlier had earned a $10,000 salary were likely to be earning $20,000-$25,000 in commissions in 1986 if they made the transition successfully. Commissions were not capped but were somewhat limited by the nature and cost of basic banking services. The big payoff for the branch sales force, Puckett suggested, will come when banks get additional products which can be directly sold. "We're building with new products in mind. We'll be ready," he asserted.

◇

On October 29, 1983, Central lost Hugh Daniel, who died at 77 after a long illness. His withdrawal from the bank had been gradual. He relinquished the chairmanship in 1975 and became a director emeritus in April 1980, although he continued to attend board meetings from time to time through 1982. The bank had long since ceased to depend on Daniel in a major, practical way, but he had loomed so large in its early success and had become such a fast friend to Brock that his passing was felt as a significant loss. It was a serious intrusion of mortality, the first sign that the age of the Titans was ending. There are few $3-billion banks whose founders still walk the streets, but now Daniel, the oldest of the originators, was the first to go.

Before Daniel's death, Brock partly repaid his friend for all his help in launching Central. When the Fluor Corp. and the Greenville Daniels were negotiating the sale of Daniel International to Fluor in 1977, Hugh Daniel, slowed by a serious stroke, asked Brock, who was also a director of the Daniel company, to fight it. It was impossible to block the sale, Brock found, but he worked closely with Daniel's wife, Martha Stone Cobb Daniel, and his son, Bill. They were able to negotiate a higher price for the company and the division of the Daniel Foundation, bringing half of it to Alabama. Under Mrs. Daniel's control, it became, by the end of 1985, one of the two largest foundations in the state. When Daniel died, Brock and Mrs. Daniel were named co-executors. So closely linked are the interests of the Daniels and Central Bank that half the assets of the Daniel Foundation in 1986 consisted of Central Bank stock.

◇

One unexpected tribute to Central's success arrived with the shareholder proxy cards in March 1983. Scrawled in shaky handwriting on one of the cards was this message: "In my judgment you and your officers have done a superior job with this bank since you got control." It was signed by shareholder William H. Ellis, who had fought so hard to block the State National merger in 1969. *Ellis v. State National* was resolved at last.

◇

By the mid '80s, Central was on a more conservative, even more conventional business tack. Asset growth slowed to 4.2 percent in 1983, 9.7 percent in 1984, and 6.7 percent in 1985 but rose by 16.6 percent in 1986. Deposits actually declined by 6.5 percent in 1983. Brannon talked philosophically of Central's earlier need for growth and its present need to emphasize profits. A solid financial performance after 1981, a robust bull market and a general return to favor of bank stocks among investors helped to push the price of Central's stock, which split two-for-one again in October 1985 and then three-for-two in October 1986, to $22.25 a share by February 1987, its highest price to date. Bill Daniel's $10,000 gamble had paid off at $667,500, and Brock's initial stock option was worth almost $6.7 million. Major mergers continued to be the province of its rivals, as Central settled solidly into fourth place in size among the major Alabama bank holding companies.

1986 Year-End Assets

AmSouth	$5.9 billion
SouthTrust	$5.1 billion
First Alabama	$4.4 billion
Central	$3.8 billion

CHAPTER ELEVEN

The Long Road To Merger

IF 1981 WAS A DISAPPOINTMENT from an earnings standpoint, it also brought one of Central's brightest successes and the happy culmination of a struggle that had gone on for thirteen and a half years. The two banks, Central of Birmingham and the old State National of Decatur, were finally able to effect the merger that had so alarmed Alabama bankers in 1968.

Forming Central Bancshares as a multibank holding company had always been Brock's second choice. He never quite forgave the court for blocking his merger, and in the lobbying frenzy of 1969, he had memorized the way from Birmingham to Montgomery. Back-slapping and arm-twisting had entered quickly into his bloodstream. Furthermore, he found it vaguely offensive that laws would prohibit a business from going to customers who would welcome it and use its services. What he wanted philosophically was unrestricted branch banking — the opportunity for a bank to go anywhere in the state (or eventually in the nation) where it could make money by offering something people wanted. So he set out to change the law, even though Central stood to gain less from statewide branching than its major competitors. (They were stronger retail banks with larger branching systems, and were more willing bidders for banks in new markets.)

Brock knew he was firing the first, largely symbolic shot of a long campaign. But he did feel certain that time was on his side and that some day he would win. That time was not the early 1970s. Central's first attempt was soundly defeated. The large banks, natural allies in an effort to expand branching rights, remained faintly hostile to the idea. The independent bankers were openly hostile. They were aroused, organized, and eager to settle the score for 1969. So Brock issued his challenge, took his wallop and limped off to plan for the next time.

Before legislative sessions, Brock would get together with Central's counsel — James Hancock initially, but soon Paul Jones of the Balch, Bingham, Baker law firm — to plan the upcoming strategy. Jones would draft the bills. Sometimes they would call for statewide branching, sometimes for the right to merge affiliates of a holding company into a single bank with all offices operated as branches. Sometimes they modestly went after only the right to branch into metropolitan areas. Sometimes Brock and Jones tried more than one bill per session. "This went on for so long that the bills all started to run together," Jones reflects, rubbing his head. "Every regular session we would drop in a handful of bills, but nothing would ever happen."

Through 1978, as Jones recalls it, no Central branch banking bill was ever passed by even one house of the legislature. Recognizing a stalemate, Brock tried to bury the hatchet. He met with leaders of the independent bankers to try to find a bill they would not oppose, but the independent bankers were suspicious, and it was difficult to find leaders who could really speak for the independents. Once, Jones says, "we seemed to have reached a compromise on branching, but it unraveled." Negotiations were no more successful than lobbying.

Actually, Central was making slight progress, losing by less overwhelming margins each year as Brock and Jones were able to win a few converts to their way of thinking.

The tide of battle turned dramatically in 1979, when a merger bill, which would have allowed holding companies to convert their own affiliate banks into branches without losing branching rights, actually passed the Alabama Senate. Attention swiftly shifted to the House, and Central, sniffing victory, adrenaline pumping, went into action. Brock and Jones worked the legislature like fanatics. Carolyn Robertson has vivid memories of the summer of 1979 — standing in her kitchen in robe and slippers at 11 o'clock at night, receiving frequent reports and requests from Brock and placing calls all over the state in an attempt to mobilize support for the bill. Brock or Jones would approach a key legislator, who would often mention a specific community banker or two from his district, bankers who would have to give him the green light before he would feel ready to vote for the bill. So Robertson would try to reach the banker if he had strong ties to Central. If he didn't, the hunt was on to find a friendly businessman who was a customer of that banker and ask him to call the banker, all to try to persuade the banker that he would not be harmed by the legislation, that he should allow it to move forward.

On the other side, Robert Cleckler remembers getting a frantic call from the independent bankers to come to Montgomery. Cleckler was the Wallace superintendent of banking who had put Central in business by approving Schuyler Baker's charter. Cleckler had served in three cabinets in Montgomery and was a popular, influential man with excellent contacts. And he was chairman of the $18-million First National Bank of Childersburg. He liked Brock and Central, but this was an independent banker cause, and he was an independent banker. By Cleckler's account, he arrived in Montgomery to find that Central had the votes to get the bill passed by the House — narrowly. He went to work, calling in political IOUs and visiting old friends. He was able to change enough votes, he says, to tip the balance. When the House voted in late July 1979, the bill was defeated by two votes, 50-48, with seven members not voting.

The defeat was crushing, Robertson remembers, but also promising. By coming so close, Central had sent out a message that someday soon it was going to win. The independent bankers got the message. So did the large bank holding companies. Negotiations now began in earnest. The heads of the holding companies began to meet regularly to discuss their common interests. In December 1980, they formed the Modern Banking Association; one of the first items on its agenda was a merger bill. Holding company representatives began to meet with the independent bankers, a few of whom had their own interests in being able to merge some small independent banks. The holding companies were willing to compromise. The independents asked for, and got, a provision that banks that were converted into branches would lose their right to create additional branches within their home counties for two years after merger.

By the time the legislature convened in 1981, the six holding companies were lined up together in support of a merger bill, and the independents were offering no organized opposition. "We met at First Alabama Bank one night and worked out what we would agree to," recalls Gene Faulkner, president of the $21-million Citizens Bank of Prattville and one of the small bank leaders. "They never could have passed it without our cooperation. They only got what we agreed to. Harry Brock even told us, 'I know we can't pass anything that you object to,' " he insists.

The vote itself, coming in the spring of 1981, was anti-climactic. It sailed through the Senate on April 28 without attracting a negative vote, although a number of senators abstained. On May 6, it passed the House handily, with only eight votes against it. It was duly signed into law by Governor Fob James.

That law, like most of the legislation for increased banking powers and greater freedom for branching and mergers, was drafted at Central Bank by Paul Jones and his staff. Central was literally rewriting the banking laws of Alabama.

The Governor's signature had barely dried when Central filed applications with the bank regulators to consolidate its affiliate banks. By December 1981, the necessary approvals had been issued, and Central combined ten of its 12 affiliates into a single bank. In 1969, the near-merger of Central and State National almost created a $305-million bank, the third largest in the state, still behind the $634-million First of Birmingham and the $343-million Birmingham Trust. In 1981, the combination of Central's banks in Birmingham, Decatur, Montgomery, Auburn, Jasper, Eufaula, Tuscaloosa, Uniontown, Dothan and Springville created a $2.2-billion bank. It was the largest in Alabama, bigger even than the almighty $1.7-billion First of Birmingham. They had done it. They were merged at last, and they were number one. It was the happy culmination to a struggle that had gone on for thirteen and a half years. The exultation contrasted sharply with the anxiety and tension over the dismal earnings of 1981, which hit an all-time low at about the same time the merger went through. But the exultation was real.

Brock put up a large sign at the entrance to the Central Penthouse, the fourteenth floor area where large parties and important meetings were often held. It read, "Welcome to Central Bank, Alabama's largest bank." It was there for John Woods, the chairman and chief executive of AmSouth, First of Birmingham's holding company, to see when he came to a meeting at Central. "Let me know, John, when I should take down my sign," Woods remembers Brock teasing him. It would be another year and a half before AmSouth was ready to merge its affiliates and force Brock to take down his sign. First Alabama did merge most of its affiliates, but not until the mid 1980s and not until Frank Plummer had retired. By mid-1986, SouthTrust had barely begun the merger process. It is a complex, time-consuming business to merge a group of banks, and the other major bank holding companies went about it cautiously and deliberately, but Central, as usual, was in a hurry.

CHAPTER TWELVE

Forging A Corporate Culture

BECAUSE ITS LIFESPAN has been brief and intense, Central Bank, more conspicuously than most companies, has a clear corporate culture, almost a personality. Years of selling and promoting, of accommodation and invention to satisfy customers, of publicizing its achievements to gain recognition, of finding and exploiting the levers of power and of being scorned and ostracized by the banking community have made Central a "character" among banks.

Few banks as large as Central are as forthrightly entrepreneurial. It is not run by caretaker managers with professional detachment. The boss is the largest shareholder; he built his personal fortune by building the bank, and his wealth still consists primarily of Central stock. Stock options figured largely in the compensation of other senior officers. Virtually no decision is made at Central that does not consider the interests of shareholders.

This circumstance has not produced a bank that is cautious, protective of its spreads or distinguished by a big return on equity. Nor has it produced an owners' bank with a customers-be-damned attitude. In fact, the entrepreneurial hustle to build the bank drove Central to find ways to serve customers who weren't being accommodated by other banks and to keep its loan rates as low as it prudently could. One result was economic growth for Alabama, which made everyone a winner. Rivals now acknowledge that competition from Central produced a more competitive, more economically useful banking industry for the state. Brock takes real pride in the economic benefits that extended from Central. "We were not altruistic in our motives, but we produced a noble result," he says. Founding director Wendell Taylor remembers something Brock explained before Central ever opened its doors: "It's a two-way street. You have to serve the people so that as they become more successful, you'll be more successful, too."

Brock and Central can now bask in general praise and recognition for revolutionizing banking in Alabama. Guy Caffee has retired but, as the chief executive of SouthTrust for many years, he slugged it out with Brock and Central in the marketplace. He offers this observation of Brock: "He unquestionably stirred up the banking community with his techniques and approaches. Like Mills B. Lane in Atlanta, he was good for banking. I know the bank I ran grew faster then than it had ever grown before. It meant that the public was served better, and it was also good for bank shareholders. They fared better because the bankers were working harder."

An observation by the late Frank Samford, one of Birmingham's leading businessmen and the former chief executive of Torchmark Corporation, is typical of how Central is viewed by the city's business community: "Central was a very aggressive bank and woke up the other banks a little — got them on the ball. It was a positive force." Notes Kenneth McCartha, Alabama's superintendent of banking from 1978 to 1985, "Birmingham was a very conservative market, but Brock and Central changed all that. I've listened to bankers who were not particular friends of Central admit that it was Brock who got banking on the move. He's still doing it." The same message comes from Jon Burke, bank stock analyst and first vice president of Robinson-Humphrey/American Express: "It's often been said that a lot of the economic development of Atlanta was due to an aggressive group of bankers, notably Mills B. Lane. Credit is the grease of economic development. In Alabama before Central Bank, the banks were conservative and didn't make many loans, particularly to entrepreneurs. If nobody makes those loans, it hurts the chances for prosperity. The people at Central made a difference in the economy of Alabama, even though they didn't have the best bank to do it with."

As State Representative Jimmy Clark, an acknowledged Central partisan, sees it, "Harry had an early grasp of what was going to take place in banking, and he put Central on the leading edge, way out ahead of almost everyone else. He was for stimulating business activity in Alabama with more aggressive banking. Others, mostly managers, were for treading water." Former newspaper editor John Bloomer, whose distaste for George Wallace led him to refuse to buy Central stock and who is therefore no fan, observes, "Central Bank has been the most dynamic financial institution in the state and one which, through original action, has brought about great changes in our banking business."

Brock takes such accolades as welcome vindication of an enterprise that so many criticized, but such praise does not mean that Central is now a member in good standing of the Alabama bankers' club. Central is certainly less an outcast than it was in 1969, but differences remain. Brock brandishes a Birmingham newspaper containing a large ad in which Central recognizes special efforts by employees that kept the bank open during a bad 1985 snowstorm. Across the bottom, in heavy type, it concludes, "ANOTHER REASON TO SWITCH TO CENTRAL." "The other banks don't like this kind of thing," he explains. "We'll have to give this up if we ever want to join the fraternity. Maybe some day we will."

Partly out of haste in its scramble to grow quickly with limited resources, and partly from its can-do ethic of finding ways to satisfy customers and get the job done, Central developed a reputation as a pragmatic bank. "Harry is more pragmatic than some of us," First Alabama's Jack Hurley diplomatically explains. Rival Caffee is more blunt: "He doesn't care whose toes he steps on to get to his goal." Says Wallace Malone, a longtime rival who now heads SouthTrust, "Brock is highly political and has a reputation of doing whatever he wants and worrying about the regulations later."

Such controversy over Central's methods is diminishing, partly because many of the things Central did that once raised eyebrows are now commonly accepted and even praised by traditional banks. What was once frowned upon as "buying business" is now considered "vigorous competition." Where once any political involvement would taint a bank, banks now pour money into political action committees and time and energy into direct lobbying. Central remains an organization that recognizes the value of power and influence and seeks to find such levers and use them to the bank's advantage, but so do its rivals now.

The easy equation of Central Bank with Harry Brock is commonplace and revealing. Baker's original offer to build a bank around Brock like a tailor fitting him with a suit of clothes came to pass to a greater extent than either of them expected, and Brock owns Central as few individuals can own a $3-billion bank. He is its largest individual shareholder, but Central belongs to Brock more completely than stock alone can measure. His essential dominance of the organization has colored its efforts to develop a management team.

Top managers are necessarily Brock's choices and likely to reflect his attraction to entrepreneurial personalities and to people who are tremendously committed to the cause. Central has a reputation as a fun place to work and a bank that will pay top dollar for top talent. Few banking organizations have rewarded their executives with better wealth-building opportunities than Central. Good pay, stock options, ambitious goals and a larger-than-normal amount of freedom to succeed or fail have caused a fair share of fast-track professionals to come and go from Central over the years.

Management arrangements at Central have reflected Brock's heavy emphasis on motivation, his conviction that competition brings out the best in people, and his concern that stagnation breeds complacency. Brock has tended to keep the pot stirred, and Central's management tree has been written in pencil.

Brock stirred the pot vigorously in 1980 by recruiting Philip C. Jackson, Jr., a former Birmingham mortgage banker and past president of the Mortgage Bankers Association of America who had served as a governor of the Federal Reserve System from 1975-78. He brought to Central prestige, a national reputation and solid contacts in both Alabama and Washington. Jackson was named chairman and CEO of the Birmingham bank and vice chairman of the holding company. Following the merger of the Central banks in 1981, he remained vice chairman. Jackson's reputation was particularly useful in correspondent banking, and he was able to help Central launch a credible national accounts department.

Two other relatively young men have risen conspicuously to the top level of senior executives. Paul Jones, the bank's principal outside legal counsel at Balch, Bingham, Baker, came inside in 1978 and joined the executive group as senior vice president and general counsel, rising to executive vice president in 1980, then to vice chairman in 1984. Dan Puckett, who joined the organization in early 1970 as an investment officer at State National Bank in Decatur, prior to the holding company formation, moved steadily up through the ranks, working within and then managing the prestigious investment division for a while, then heading Central's north Alabama bank (relocated from Decatur to Huntsville) before returning to Birmingham in 1982 and joining Brock, Brannon, Jackson and Jones on the senior policy committee as executive vice president in 1984.

For all its disrespectful overturning of banking traditions, Central harbors a fond attachment to its own traditions. It is full of a sense that it has made history. Scrapbooks filled with press clippings dating back to the bank's first public appearances are carefully maintained. Anecdotes of Brock, Tate and the old days still circulate. While the bank has become huge, modern and institutional, there is a strong effort to hold onto the excitement, intensity and personal commitment of the early days. It has outrun the expectations of its founders, but it clings to their original values. Notes Doug Mims, who has had ample opportunity to see Central from the inside and the outside, "The one thread that runs throughout Central's history is 'get off your rear end and go out and ask for the business.' "

EPILOGUE

Forward Into An Interstate Era

A GREAT DEAL of management time at Central, as in most major banks throughout the country during the 1980s, has been spent preparing for interstate banking. True to its colors, Central was an early and staunch advocate of interstate banking, even though many observers predicted that none of Alabama's banking companies would be large enough to dominate a major interstate system and keep its headquarters in Alabama. Brock has insisted for years that he did not intend to take orders from Atlanta, but he advocated interstate banking in the name of unfettered competition. Then he took steps to see that he would have to take orders from Atlanta only on his own terms, if at all.

The prospect of interstate mergers created a more aggressive climate for bank acquisitions, and unfriendly takeover attempts became less rare than they were when Brock surprised State National in 1968. Unfriendly takeovers have been attempted in Florida, and unsolicited offers have sparked bidding wars in Georgia, Virginia and the Carolinas. The back door was now wide open for acquirers to bypass management and appeal directly to shareholders.

Brock had no intention of letting anyone do unto him as he had once done, and he knew in 1981, with Central's battered stock selling at half its book value, that he was vulnerable to "someone coming in and stealing this bank out from under us." So Central in 1982 moved to put in place what Jones calls, "state-of-the-art shark repellent." Changes in the charter and by-laws made it difficult for a would-be acquirer to buy a significant amount of stock without offering the same price to all shareholders.

"Central is reasonably bulletproof now, with charter shark repellent and over 40 percent of the stock owned by officers and directors or in other very friendly hands," notes Jon Burke, a bank stock analyst for Robinson-Humphrey/American Express. "Such a combination makes it very difficult to acquire the bank without the blessing of the insiders."

With their defense in place, Central's management turned its attention to offense. Central executives had consistently said for years that they intended to be an acquirer in interstate banking, while conceding that "at the right price, anything sells" — even Central. Brock's ambition is transparent: he wants to go out, when he retires, as head of an interstate banking organization.

He threw Central's weight behind passage by the Alabama legislature of a regional, reciprocal interstate banking bill that would bring Alabama into the banking region created by Georgia, Florida, the Carolinas, Virginia and Tennessee, allowing Alabama bank holding companies to acquire banks in those states and vice versa. Central was not alone this time but marched arm in arm with AmSouth. Still, they were thwarted for some time by opposition from a Wallace Malone-led SouthTrust and certain independent banks. The outlook was still bleak enough in 1985 for AmSouth to terminate its 1984 "cross-investment" arrangement with major banks in Georgia and South Carolina, a tentative plan for future interstate affiliation, in light of the unwillingness of the Alabama legislature to authorize such arrangements. The discouraging political prospects sent Central in search of a back door or an unlocked window.

Such openings existed. One prominent loophole surfaced in 1984, when the Comptroller of the Currency began to approve charters for bank holding companies to form "nonbank banks" (banks which forgo either commercial loans or regular checking accounts) in states other than their home states. Central quickly filed five applications for consumer banks in Atlanta; Kensington, Md.; and Orlando, St. Petersburg and Fort Lauderdale, Fla. Litigation obstructed this avenue for expansion, and even a unanimous Supreme Court decision in favor of nonbank banks in January 1986 failed to rekindle enthusiasm for this option at Central. Interest had shifted elsewhere.

Even back in 1984, the nonbank bank applications were a minor diversion for Jones and his legal department. Central had a really big bombshell on the boards, and excitement ran high in late 1984 among the few executives who knew about the top-priority project.

A few outsiders had caught wind of the idea, however, and in late November 1984, Atlanta bank stock analyst Jon Burke could grin cryptically and say, "I assure you that the entrepreneurial spirit is alive and well in Harry Brock." He had learned about the plan from the number-one news leaker in the Central organization, Brock himself, that Central was preparing to renounce its bank charter to become an S&L. Savings and loans were a seriously ill industry in 1984 as a consequence of the high interest rates. To keep as many of them afloat as possible, Congress and the regulators had showered them with exemptions and privileges. It was much easier for an S&L to branch at will and to develop an interstate system than for a bank to do so. Capital requirements were extremely liberal and rigged to help keep marginal thrifts open. Even more important, S&L powers had expanded tremendously. An S&L could do most of the things that a bank could do and a great deal that a bank could not do. S&Ls had the insurance powers, the real estate powers and the investment powers that banks were clamoring for. Hundreds of bankers objected to the competitive advantages enjoyed by S&Ls, and bank regulators observed that, under current law, an S&L charter was the ticket to have. There was no question that a high-spirited entrepreneur would be much freer to roam and compete as he wanted to if he had an S&L charter instead of a bank charter. In fact, applications for new S&L charters ran high, but no major, mainstream commercial bank had ever converted to an S&L.

Central was giving the move extremely careful consideration. For a while it looked to the insiders as if Brock would throw the dice. In the end, he held onto them, wary of the damage the bombshell would do to Central's own intricate structure of accounts. There were troublesome limits on the amounts and types of commercial loans an S&L could hold, and an S&L still could not offer commercial checking accounts. There was too much value in Central's commercial checking accounts to justify the move, Brock concluded. It was a price Central could not bring itself to pay, so with a sigh, Brock set the plan aside and Central searched for other ways to get around the competitive restrictions that were hemming the company in.

The real break in the geographic restrictions came in 1985, when the opponents of regional interstate banking bowed to mounting pressure and eroding support and gave up their opposition in return for a delayed implementation date of July 1, 1987. AmSouth had publicly led the charge this time as Brock, still a polarizing figure among Alabama bankers, lay low and Paul Jones represented Central. Directors of both AmSouth and Central were active among legislators, campaigning for votes for a bill that would make Alabama an active player in the interstate banking region in the Southeast, an idea which was becoming increasingly irresistible in state after state. These directors, Brock suggests, also made low-key contacts with their counterparts at First Alabama and SouthTrust, hinting at the economic folly of sitting out the move to interstate banking or arriving after the game was nearly over.

A few community bankers made noises about opposing any form of interstate banking, but essentially in Alabama, as elsewhere, the small banks were inclined to be neutral and not highly interested in what they considered a family affair among big banks. Finally, at the August 1985 board meeting of the Modern Banking Association, which had been split by the division among its principal members, SouthTrust dropped its opposition and the political wheels began to turn smoothly. The measure passed the Alabama senate on January 28, 1986, by a 30-0 vote, sailed through the House on February 20 by a 90-1 margin and was signed into law that same day by Governor Wallace. Central and AmSouth had their tickets, dated July 1, 1987, to the regional interstate ballgame.

This was the front door Central really wanted to use for its interstate expansion. Brock was talking enthusiastically in early 1987 about out-of-state acquisitions of banks smaller than Central in growing markets throughout the South.

Central would be a survivor, he insisted, and could profitably compete with larger organizations. Central would accept only minimal dilution in such mergers — nothing the bank couldn't earn its way out of in three years, Brock insisted.

Central's actual break through the boundaries of Alabama came in February 1987 in a sudden, unexpected way that took even Central's interstate scouts by surprise. On Thursday, February 19, Jones took a call from the Atlanta office of the FDIC, which was shopping for buyers for three small banks it would have to close. One was in Oklahoma; another was 80 miles southwest of Lubbock, Texas. Jones yawned. The third was the First National Bank of Crosby, Texas, 21 miles east of Houston. Jones leaned forward in his chair. Was it, he asked, in the same county as Houston? Could it, under Texas law, branch into Houston? The FDIC caller checked it out and got back to him: it was, and it could.

Central quickly put together its first bid on a failing interstate bank. At 5 percent of deposits, roughly the going rate, the price came to a little over $400,000, so that is what Central bid. From all Central could see, the Crosby bank was attracting little interest from other bidders, so the Central team was not surprised to hear on February 26 that the bank was theirs.

It was at once a very modest and a rather bold stroke. Central had bought one of the smallest, cheapest tickets imaginable into what Jones called, "a market that, even on a bad day, is bigger than the state of Alabama." Two weeks earlier, Central people had been scouting Dallas, talking to some larger, healthier banks there. Now Houston had been offered to them for a song. Central's Texas strategy was still embryonic when this history went to press, but there was no doubt that Central was going for a slice of the Houston market and planned to get it with a low overhead shop that could afford to gather funds by paying top rates and would then seek to expand its toehold in the loan market with aggressive marketing.

"We hadn't planned this one, but it fits our strategy very well," Jones explained. "We want to go in small and then build through penetration. Without much real estate and fancy furnishings, this bank presented very low fixed overhead costs. We didn't have to pay for things we didn't want and wouldn't use. It gave us a unique opportunity to enter that market, and we took it." It was a promising start.

◇

Central is a dynamic organization scrambling through dynamic times. It has come far during its brief lifetime, anticipating change, causing change, profiting from change. Its future is not assured and cannot be, but its future is promising because banking is headed toward increased competition, rapid adaptation, marketing responsiveness, entrepreneurial leadership and increased dependence on selling products — all fields in which Central excels. Central might go out in a blaze of entrepreneurial glory not too many years from now, shrewdly bartered away in exchange for a wonderful premium for its shareholders. It might, in its maturity and Brock's, settle down to a profitable respectability and eventually join the banking fraternity. But it also might continue to leap in astonishing, unexpected ways. Its written history, therefore, cannot yet be concluded, only suspended.

About the Author

Richard H. Gamble is a financial journalist based in Atlanta who has written extensively about banks and banking. From 1977 to 1985, he was editor of *The Southern Banker;* he is presently editor of *CASHFLOW,* a magazine for corporate treasurers. He received M.A. and Ph.D. degrees from the University of Pittsburgh, has taught in college programs in Iowa, Illinois and Pennsylvania and held a post-doctoral research fellowship at the Newberry Library in Chicago.

Chronology

July 1955	Harry Brock returns to Alabama from New York, joins Exchange Security Bank
June 1963	Schuyler Baker talks to Brock about starting a new bank
December 31, 1963	Brock hired as general manager
March 2, 1964	Central Bank & Trust opens its doors
September 1964	Merger agreement announced between State National Bank in Decatur and First National Bank of Gadsden
April 1965	Central sells 100,000 shares of stock at $5 each
November 1965	Central sells 100,000 shares of stock at $10 each
August 11, 1966	Central opens its second and third branches on the same day
October 29, 1967	New headquarters opens on S. 20th Street
July 9, 1968	State National board authorizes merger negotiations with the Morrows
July 11, 1968	Phone call from Hugh Agricola to Brock starts scramble for State National stock
July 15, 1968	Brock goes to Decatur to announce takeover
July 19, 1968	Morrows make tender offer for State National at $80 a share
July 20, 1968	Brock counters with offer at $80-85 a share
September 16, 1968	Central and State National boards fail to reach merger agreement at joint meeting
December 13, 1968	Central and State National boards adopt merger plan

January 10, 1969	Lawsuit (*Ellis v. State National*) filed to block merger
January 15, 1969	AlaBA executive committee votes to seek legislation to block merger, multibank holding companies
January 28, 1969	Shareholders of Central and State National approve merger by a large margin
May 20, 1969	Bills introduced in state legislature to block merger, multibank holding companies
June 2, 1969	Two-day trial begins before Judge Thomas
June 17, 1969	Judge Thomas rules against Central, blocking the merger
June 19, 1969	State National board, over Brock's objections, votes to abandon merger and seek a holding company
July 30, 1969	Senate Banking Committee holds hearings on the block-Brock bill
September 4, 1969	Alabama legislature adjourns without enacting legislation to block merger, multibank holding companies
September 23, 1969	Newspaper account links First National of Montgomery, Exchange Security and First National of Huntsville in multibank holding company talks
October 1969	Brock named "consultant" to State National, takes staff position there
January 27, 1970	State National board enlarged by 12 new members
July 3, 1970	Application filed to form First Alabama Bancshares as the state's first multibank holding company
September 1970	Hearings in Birmingham air opposition to First Alabama application
October 28, 1970	U.S. Court of Appeals upholds Judge Thomas
December 8, 1970	State National board balks at 5-to-1 exchange ratio in holding company plan

December 12, 1970	Central files multibank holding company application
December 15, 1970	State National board votes 17-3 for an exchange ratio of 5.5-to-1
December 18, 1970	State National board votes 19-5 to accept holding company plan with 5-to-1 exchange ratio
April 21, 1971	Fed votes 5-2 to approve First Alabama application
May 13, 1971	Hearings in Birmingham on Central application
July 13, 1971	First Alabama becomes state's first multibank holding company
July 27, 1971	U.S. Supreme Court refuses to hear Central's appeal
October 8, 1971	Fed votes 4-3 to approve Central application
December 20, 1971	Central and State National Corp. becomes state's second multibank holding company
February 3, 1972	Alabama Bancorporation (later AmSouth) becomes third multibank holding company
December 6, 1972	Alabama Financial Group (later SouthTrust) becomes fourth multibank holding company
January 23, 1973	Central and State National Corp. changes name to Central Bancshares of the South, Inc.
April 19, 1973	Central sells stock at $26.50 per share in public offering
January 1975	Clyde Tate departs Central, plans to start rival bank
September 27, 1977	Brock escapes serious injury in plane crash that kills pilot
July 1979	State House of Representatives defeats merger bill, 50-48

May 6, 1981	State House passes merger bill with only eight negative votes
December 1981	Central merges affiliates to become largest bank in Alabama at $2.2 billion

Index

— C —

— D —

— K —

— L —

— M —

— N —

— O —

— P —

— R —

— S —